IMANIMAN

POETS WRITING IN THE ANZALDÚAN BORDERLANDS

EDITED BY

ire'ne lara silva and Dan Vera

Introduction by Juan Felipe Herrera

aunt lute books

San Francisco

Aunt Lute Books
P.O. Box 410687
San Francisco, CA 94141
www.auntlute.com

Cover design: Amy Woloszyn, Amymade Graphic Design
Text design: Andrea Ikeda
Senior Editor: Joan Pinkvoss
Managing Editor: Shay Brawn
Production: Andrea Ikeda, Micaela Clark, Ali Giordani, Kari Simonsen, Maya Sisneros, and Taylor Hodges

Library of Congress Cataloging-in-Publication Data

Names: Silva, Ire'ne Lara, editor. | Vera, Dan, editor. | Herrera, Juan
    Felipe, writer of introduction.
Title: Imaniman : poets writing in the Anzaldúan borderlands / edited by
    Ire'ne Lara Silva and Dan Vera ; introduction by Juan Felipe Herrera.
Description: San Francisco : Aunt Lute Books, 2016.
Identifiers: LCCN 2016042003 | ISBN 9781879960930 (acid-free paper)
Subjects: LCSH: Southwest, New--Literary collections. | American
    literature--Southwest, New. | Anzaldúa, Gloria,--Influence.
Classification: LCC PS566 .I45 2016 | DDC 810.8/0979--dc23
LC record available at https://lccn.loc.gov/2016042003

Printed in the U.S.A. on acid-free paper

10 9 8 7 6 5 4 3 2 1

Contents

Contents

IMANIMAN

POETS WRITING IN THE
ANZALDÚAN BORDERLANDS

Anzaldúa Lives On ─────────
Poetry, Transformations & Flashes into the Serpent Eye

Juan Felipe Herrera
Poet Laureate of the United States

Anzaldúa lives on:

lesbian leader,
> borderlands genius, thinker &
>> writer woman of the skull-belt
>>> crystals of the Mexica sacred stone serpent figure, Coatlicue.

Here, those ancient Nahuatl death-rebirth crystals, stones, claws, bones — that which holds, transforms — & findings unfold & speak through cantos, letters, testimonials, multi-visions & multi-genres. Within shifting borders — it is good to enter into these voice worlds — to stand, bow & listen in their presence. Peoples, familias, cities, towns, rancherías and the wilderness of all border-crossers & messengers of border spaces open in these pages.

I am moved by these inner and outer voyages —

(almost half a century ago with the new Raza of UCLA, at Royce Quad Library, we used to check out all the books from F1219.00 to F1235.00, drag them back to our apartments in Westwood, Santa Monica & East LA, listen to Santana, listen to Pharoah Sanders & listen-listen as we hit hard dirt & backyard rock outside planting maize on impossible dirt — these volumes were the materials on Meso-America, we did not want that hyphen, we desired the fruit, the many eyes of the fruits, its own wild sisters, we wanted the frayed teachings, to soak in them and to unlock them in our very own espíritu, body-mind-word).

This collection is a signpost on the continuous journey of initial investigations into a borderless Cultura & a new power-source, an inner one, in particular one drawn from the deep vision-work of Anzaldúa —

— Anzaldúa as a pioneer-seer;
— A winding, unwinding Mano Zurda unending Bay Area workshop to the present;
— Archeologist of a New Arc, a tremulous bridge, a spine of bold conductors of consciousness;
— Keeper of a new Tucuatsi (Huichol people's term, a linguistic branch of Nahuatl),
> a radical

medicine basket of concepts, ceremonies, shaman healing word-breath-body instruments,
> language, calls & symbols & motions that can be further perceived & applied in Twenty First Century life;

— Medicine woman speaker with many voices — in one.

The healing begins with this anthology — with key questions:

How do we talk about religion & class at the same time?
Does religion end at the edge of elite class-power?
How do these things intersect?

Can the same debate be applied to the question of Color and Group Identity?

Which feels right?
— Belonging to the same-language group?
— Belonging in the same-color group or belonging in
  the same marginalized community group?
> Can you cross-over?

How about the questions of Language and Homeland:

- Can you be Brown or Black in your Brown or Black Homeland?
- Or Yellow or Red or White?
- What is speaking in "American" Black, Yellow, White, Red English?
- Let's Talk about Color: Maybe your color is shifting at every instant?
- What if there is no *color* at all? (perhaps it is a serpent-belt of life & death,
  a continuous swiveling flow larger than itself.)

> Sounds easy, odd, breaks complex.

The question of magic:
does it exist for you, what is it, where is it, can you move it? Does it have another word,
Is it *poetry, writing, Anzaldúa's Black & Red?*

Or shall we continue in a one-dimensional world —
Buying and selling, selling and buying then staring into a static nothing?
> Open these soft & hard pages. Begin your wild search.

With this collective of magnificent & brave poets & writers, let us dream-examine urban magic, race, memory, hoods & barrios, transformation, consciousness, struggle & ultimately, freedom & liberation. Can we heal subtle, fancy and long-ago border wounds (can a closed wound be an "open" wound." Is herstory a "wound."), can we carry harmony to ourselves & to the people? What people?

All — in typical Anzaldúa seriousness & laughter & new-gen mind in this anthology — let us work on it, stare into it.

Coatlicue

Rodney Gomez

Rattles delivered me. I was covered in mud. A nun.

I had my first meal in a diner on Closner Road:
chilaquiles, barbacoa, y chorizo con huevo.

Me tragué toda la basura. Me tragué la cocina y los carros.
Con gente o sin. My breath was holocaust.

I rumbled through laundromats. Sleeves of discarded uniforms
crawled to me. Soiled briefs, tattered bras, I accepted them.

Wilted sunflowers suckled at my breasts to become new again.

At night I slunk through black bars listening to the flim
of border patrol agents. They were bombardiers with no eyes.

I slept in a patchwork warehouse, drawing to me all neglected things.

The river changed its course, flowered through me.

Abandoned children were born in the entryway steps.
Children with crooked teeth, crinkled hair.
Children fueled by black holes. Drowned children & escapees.

I gave them my blood to drink.

I gave them my hands. They used them to pray.

I

A Tlamanalli for the Netted God

Daniel E. Solís y Martínez

Nomatca nehuatl/I myself.

Titlacauan
like you, we are life's slaves.
We the queer, the poor, las muxes, the feminine, the exploited, the young and
    old—the monstrous
speak to you, cuiloniteotl.
Our trickster, world shifter, hope of humanity.
Through your form—the refracted light of the Sacred All—
we find the promise of endurance and transcendence.

Cape made of stars netted with the root-rope of ceiba,
in your firm hands are shell and tobacco pipe.
At your feet rest the sacred bundles of
white sage, chichipince, jícaro, and maquilishuat,
overlooked and underestimated.
Como la maestra Gloria escribió,
your flesh is the
Darkness of Flowers.

The Netted One,
walk with us.
You hold the tobacco pipe in the left hand.
In the right, you offer us the sweet cochitzapotl for those who despair.
Beneath the chanclas on your feet,
the ghostly threshold to the nine plains lays open
tempting us with the cloying nectar of resignation and defeat.
We cling to your netted cape as we leap
into the whirlwinds,
praying that we land on the firm earth.

Smooth, worn clean by the pounding ocean waves,
The shell of the Netted One rings out,
as you call back your children
to the necessary acts of survival.
Manifestation of perseverance, draw the shell to your lips,
sound your call.

We seek your guidance,
Entangled One.
Give us the facultad to perceive the world as it is,
inhabited with ravenous sustos of desconocimientos,
wraiths stalking our every move,
seeking to devour our animas.

Titlacauan,
Tender of the Árbol de la Vida,
we honor your wisdom, whispered to us by
la maestra Gloria.
We climb the knuckled roots of
your Árbol
down into the dark, moist, ferric Earth
where the cenote waits, expectantly.

Entering through the rajaduras created
by the sinuous, searching roots,
each of must find
the shards of power within our most ancient selves,
hardforged and gifted to us by los antepasados.
We claim this birthright, the power,
To shift.
To move.
To make change.
To become change.
To forge the paths others must walk.

Darkness of Flowers,
help us remember that
each of us is made of
interwoven strands of truth and lies.
We are a tapestry
united,
tejido, strand by strand
through the compromises of every day.
The choices that carry us through,
push us forward unsure,
building a power that can allow us to withstand
what we must,
and to have the strength to do what we must:
To survive.
To become something new—
a true human being.

Titlacauan,
in the moments of fear and desperation,
remind us that through the blood and mud
caking our hands,
we are mortared to others.
Past, present and future,
all of us,
enlaced and rooted to each other.
Gift us with the understanding that
amidst the impurity of this broken world,
we create new paths fusing survival and hope,
imperfectly, but trembling with the power of transformation.

God of the Distant Shore
Who waits for us
as we wade through the blood-stained water,
guide us into the unseen night, together.

Redeemer of the world,
we call to you.

The Netted One,
Guardian of the Tangled Paths,
Holder of the Days,
Keeper of the Ceiba Stars,
Master of the Reed Dance,
Tender of the Árbol de la Vida,
Cihuātlahtoāni of Nepantla,
Greenskeeper of the Seeds Within,
The mesh upholding the world,
The compromised one,
The impure one,
The entangler,
The survivor,
The strength within us as we do what must be done,
The redeemer of the day yet to dawn.

Tahui, tahui, tahui, tahui.

I wrote this ofrenda/offering to the compromised god, Titlacauan, because in my spiritual practices he embodies a way to make sense of the daily contradictions I am forced into because this world is broken. Titlacauan is an ancient god. He is the trickster aspect of the powerful Nahua god of magicks, obsidian, war, and co-creator of the world, Tezcatlipoca; a member of the sacred triad of Quetzalcoatl and Huitzilopochtli. Titlacauan in the Nahua language means, "We are his slaves."

In the thinking of Nahua peoples throughout present-day Mexico and Central America, Titlacauan was a divine pathway for ordinary people to gain power over the omnipotent Tezcatlipoca by containing him. This containment took many forms, from the net cape the Titlacauan was shown wearing, to the ritualized insults that were hurled at him when a supplicant needed healing. But the primary mechanism every day Nahuas used to gain power over the forces of their worlds, was through the metaphorical sexual penetration of the god Titlacauan. Called a cuiloni—or penetrated man—Titlacauan was a means of empowerment for normally oppressed Nahua people. To symbolically fuck the god allowed Nahua individuals to assert a measure of power over the uncontrollable and have a chance to make real their will in the world. By invoking Titlacauan in the times they were facing overwhelming forces and barriers such as famine, war, pestilence, and hurricanes, people could claim some power over the divine forces that rule this world.

While at first glance this conceptualization of Titlacauan might appear patriarchal and heterosexist, in my thinking, it instead offers up a model for a power that lies in the margins. Titlacauan, as an idea of the divine, offers a radically different way to think about what power is and how those of us who live beyond this world's boundaries can find the power we need to enact transformative healing. Titlacauan's power is the power of the fucked, the bottom, the oppressed.

I am guided in this thinking by key parts of the powerful constellations of ideas generated by Gloria E. Anzaldúa. The idea of nepantla—a space/time of transformative potential that can be used by people to recreate themselves into warrior-healers capable of making a new, whole, and just world—grounds several of Anzaldúa's concepts: árbol de la vida, el cenote, la facultad, and sustos de desconocimientos. As Anzaldúa, and those who have followed her, conceptualized nepantla, it is a place that allows endurance of life's injustice (sustos de desconocimientos) by guiding its denizens towards transformation at the conscious and unconscious planes (el cenote), through the lodestar of hope. In surviving the acts of oppression, a person can use nepantla to build their skills and awareness (la facultad) to begin shifting the powers that harm them, and in communion with others construct new ways of being with others (el árbol de la vida).

For me, Titlacauan is the sacred manifestation of nepantla. He is the vessel that makes the complex and chaotic space of nepantla comprehensible. In my daily life, through his form and symbolism, I feel the power of chaos and change and am able to grasp it to overcome the forces that would destroy me. The complex terrain of my own personal relationship to the people and spiritual worldview that created Titlacauan is fraught with potential pitfalls and temptations to become a cultural appropriator, or worse, forget that I am a non-Nahua benefiting from settler colonialism on stolen Tongva and Tataviam land in what is now called Los Angeles. It is my hope that, instead, Titlacauan can be a source of power through the compromised place I occupy in this world.

Hermana in the Sky

Carmen Calatayud

I can't scrape you from my soul
or fold up your altar.
You're the sister I fought for,
grief underneath my fingernails.
Your grace engulfed me,
took me over trails
where saguaros kept our secrets
and waved us by.
With you I was explosive.
I walked with fire and water.
Now that you're gone,
I attract tricksters,
step over carcasses,
run from fists flying
toward my mouth.
I dodge the lies.
I'm lonely for friends
like lightning
that strikes my monsoon soul.

Last night I heard you weep
underneath my house.
Black bones cracked inside my throat.
You pulled me out of winter's cave,
but it's hell in the hallway
between guts and wisdom.
I'm tired of wandering
like a nomad. Aimless,
I wait for you to fly overhead.
Be my satellite. Show me where
to cross the border.

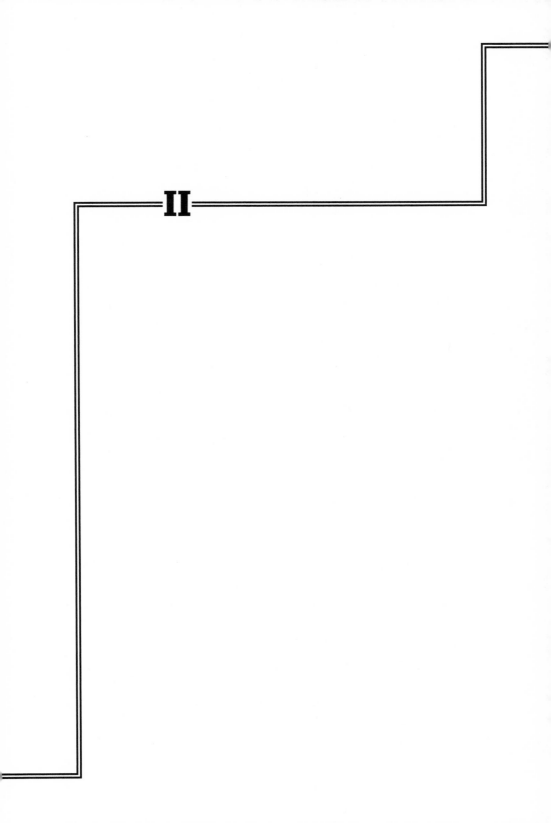

II

everything must be a little wild

ire'ne lara silva

What I've learned: I like neither lines nor boundaries nor borders. I will throw myself against the bars of even self-imposed cages. I will gnash my teeth in the face of every rule, everything I am not supposed to be or do or think or feel. I insist on sky and horizons and wind. I insist on roads and shrieking and my feet tripping towards drums. I need my tongue, split and braided and burst and transformed. I need my heart, bruised and bruta and always in tune with guitarras and rancheras. I need earth and leaves, tiny roots dripping from my hands. I need for the page to be more than the page, for words to be more than words, to speak what leaps and sparks and burns. I started writing when I was eight years old. Twenty three when I started writing with the intention of making a book. Thirty five when I held my first book. Four books to hold in my arms now. They feel like small stars, spinning in place. How odd that such small volumes hold years of my life, years of my dreaming, years of my tears and sudden inspirations. How close they came to not existing.

I only ever almost gave up once. When I was twenty eight and too many voices had named my stories *wrong/incomplete/not right/not stories*.

Putting words on a page—all words, any words—felt transgressive when I was a teenager. It was a secret language my parents couldn't unlock, a secret language my siblings had no interest in. Books were magic. That I would dare write anything was freedom and exhilaration and enough reason to endure. It didn't matter to me that every story ended in pain and death. That they modeled self-destruction again and again.

I traveled 2,000 miles to go to college. In that first year, I discovered the first Latina writers I ever read. I hadn't known they existed. I read everything, as urgently as if I was drowning and each book was precious oxygen. I saw myself reflected, refracted, expanded. I heard my languages and half languages and mixed languages, heard languages my heart remembered that I'd never heard before. I started to write, hesitantly, one line at a time.

We are made up of everywhere we have been. I am the writer I am because of what I have lived and breathed and dreamed. I am unexpected, as many Latina writers are unexpected. Some, like me, from families who could not read, without economic resources, without the education, without the identification with "American" literature. Writing has been escape and joy, pain and grief, but always a necessity.

I almost ran away from home when I was fifteen. Because my father threatened to burn all my stories and throw away the manual typewriter my mother had bought for me at the flea market. I wrote by night, in hotel restrooms with a towel under the door to hide the light. I wrote in the day, when my parents were gone and my youngest brother played. I wrote on notebooks and with pens I saved every cent of my allowance for. They were my escape my world my real life. One day my father came home unexpectedly and swept off all the papers I had on the kitchen table. I wrapped my arms around the typewriter. His arm was already raised to strike me if I took too long to move it. He demanded lunch. Threatened my things. Threatened my words. And then I knew what I had never known before. My words were mine. I would not let anyone take them. I fell asleep that night and many more with my notebooks underneath me.

Years passed. I wrote. I heard but did not listen to anything that said writing wasn't mine. That my stories were not stories. That they belonged in drawers. That no one would ever read them. I had defended my words with my body. The memory of that made my heart strong. Made my will strong. I knew very early that I was writing for myself, not to please anyone else, not for a grade, not to earn anyone's love, not to prove English was my language too, not to beg inclusion to the Western canon, not to make a marketable product, not to sell off any part of my spirit or culture in exchange for recognition.

I only heard Toni Morrison: Write what you seek and have not found. I only heard Leslie Marmon Silko: Write and heal the world. I only heard Juan Rulfo: Write language until it is fire burning the border between living and dying. I only heard Gloria Anzaldúa: Transform or die. I traveled 2,000 miles to read Anzaldúa's work, though we grew up in towns that were only twenty miles apart. Somehow, I never met her or heard her read while she was alive. It does not matter. I speak so many of her languages. She wrote so many of mine.

I looked to the sky when I wrote my stories. Not to the ground. The ground was covered in imaginary lines enforced by blood, enforced by violence, enforced by poverty. I saw no new stories on the ground. My stories were old stories and they were new stories. They bubbled up, from my bones, from my blood, from my flesh. These are the stories I always want to be writing. To tell more truth than I know that I know.

I think I'm learning light now. Light is born in giving. I am learning giving. A story must have light. Must hold light and carry light. Must demonstrate light. A story must give light. How does a story come to hold light? How does a writer learn to make a story into a vessel that invites in the light?

Light will not flow into a trapped space, a shadowed space, a space that is unknown to itself. I've spent two decades imagining freedom. Two decades telling myself I am free. Two decades trying to figure out freedom's dimensions.

I keep coming across walls that block out the light. Some I did not choose. I want those torn down. Some of them I chose when I was younger and I needed them to survive. I want those torn down. Some of them are there because I leaned on them during decades of hoping and surviving, working and working. I don't want them anymore. I built them during the seventeen years I spent as a clerical employee. And a waitress. And a housekeeper. And a caregiver. And a salesperson. And a coordinator. And a driver. I've mopped floors. I've cleaned laundromats. I've helped bathe and toilet people. I've ironed children's clothing. I've answered a million phone calls. I've typed a million million numbers a million million names a million million notes that had nothing to do with my stories.

La vida tears you into pieces. A loss here. A death there. Love come, love gone, love returned, love ended. Love never given. Love turned rock. The body wilts. An accident. An illness. A disease. Weakness and aching joints. Agony. Pain. Years pass. Dreams fray, their colors fading, the cloth thinning to transparency. You wear your dreams still, to keep you cool, to keep you warm, to tell the world you still exist.

How do we make the spirit free? Spirit without walls. Spirit without limits. I wanted to make my heart a thing with wings. No tiny flutter but the silhouette of the condor. I wanted the widest river. The trembling of the earth after thunder. Make of me a window. Make of me a door. Make of me a flower. Make of me a road. This is what I pray when I sit down to write.

There is a quote from bell hooks in *Remembered Rapture* that I've never been able to find again. Maybe I imagined it. Or thought of it while I was reading the book: that one day the writing of women of color would be revolutionary not just because it had been written by women of color but because of its content.

It is not enough to see ourselves reflected. It is not enough to speak. It is not enough to just tell our stories. It is not enough to tell our histories. It is not enough to claim the voice of the voiceless. It is not enough to send our words out into the world. The stories we tell and the consequences of those stories are our responsibility. If the stories we tell keep us in the role of victims, if the stories we tell do not speak to power, if the stories we tell re-affirm the systems and realities that oppress us, then we are not telling the stories we most urgently need.

I don't know writing that requires no effort, no strain, no heartbreak, no investment of blood and flesh and heartbreak. I don't know freedom that is obtained without endurance or kept without intention. When writers of color exist who support the dominant system, we do not have the luxury of writing without intention.

To speak against the dominant systems of power is to speak freedom. We each have our portion of free and our portion of oppressed. We struggle, in our bodies and our symbols, to nurture the free and free the oppressed. The oppressed have rage. The oppressed live in a state of competition. The common belief is that the oppressed have no gifts to give. And yet, in the soul of an artist, the foundational call is the call to give. To give of oneself, to speak of oneself. To spin in freedom, speaking self and body and spirit. The foundational call is to love, carrying and spilling out love. The foundation call is community and connection. Oppression falters when light strikes it.

It is time and time past to shed my old skins, break my old walls, birth my new hearts. I am not the lonely child, the dancing woman with the locked heart, the laborer with two decades of bread and butter jobs, the body stretched between illness and the memory of health. Not anymore.

We need the stories of transformation. The power of transformation—not dreaming it but being it, manifesting it, embodying transformation itself. The spirit requires its freedom to tell the stories that change us. The stories that are gift to the teller and to the listener. The stories that might take enough root to be passed to the following generations. Freedom is required so that a story can hold light.

We are in a time of new stories. Wounds exist at many levels. The superficial. The internal. The personal. The communal. The ancestral. A vessel that carries light can carry healing. I will always be writing healing. I must create vessels strong enough to carry light. I must be strong enough to create those vessels. The mind can become confused. The heart rarely. Las entrañas never.

We need the stories of healing. The stories that demonstrate it, that teach it. Toni Morrison said the function of freedom was to free others. I say the function of healing is to teach others to heal. Healing is the first freedom. Freedom from the wound. Freedom from victimhood. Freedom from silence. Freedom from self-injury. Freedom from self-destruction. Freedom that instructs us to love ourselves and care for ourselves. Care for our many communities. Freedom that unleashes in us the mandate to speak healing, to seed it and nurture it, until it blooms and spreads and spills.

It is my task to find the bit of light in the darkness, to shelter it in my hands until it grows stronger, to find the gleaming words that might grow to incandescence. Light cannot be an afterthought or the last plot twist. At every turn, it is necessary to dissect and rebuild stories—what we have lived, what we have read, what we have heard—every story we take in.

What I have learned—everything must be a little wild. The older I am, the more I hear myself described as ferocious. That tells me I am following my own healing and my own freedom. I have never needed a reminder that life is precarious, that no span of decades is promised. I do not know how much time I have. I have no time to waste. Healing, unleashed, is profuse and uncontrollable, re-ordering and re-shaping it as it sees fit, leaping from heart to spirit to body to mind to heart, weaving together what was torn apart. We can set no limits, no parameters, no boundaries.

Even in writing, the words leap wild. We must pursue the rough, the raw, the edges of everything. Polished writers all sound the same. What is unique is to find the wildest way we can speak, the stories with brambles and wild branches and wide, wide trunks. The stories that sing and bleed and run and burst. The stories only we can tell. The stories we are all waiting for. Stories that set the spirit free, that set the words free, that set the light free.

A Startling Illumination of Words

Tara Betts

The work of a powerful woman begets other powerful women, or that work coaxes such women out of the shadows. A powerful, innovative work inspires people who go unnamed, unrecognized, and unprivileged. Such a work can find names, languages, and myths rooted in the body, especially the brown body, and the land. When writers like Anzaldúa, Lorde, and Shange gave us autohistoria-teoría, autobiomythography, and the choreopoem, they coined a working language that shields and bolsters us in intellectual engagement because of the battle to place one's stories beyond Eurocentric, sexist, classist, and homophobic paradigms. The opposition to such ideas and practices is still very real, nuanced, and wages overt, subtle, and consistent moves against the power in such terms.

While more people of color are getting graduate degrees, educational systems are eliminating tenure and increasing the numbers of overextended adjuncts. What is becoming more evident is who is welcome to think in such institutions and who is temporarily accommodated, especially for less compensation.

Anzaldúa wrote *Borderlands* before she received her posthumously granted Ph.D. The University of California at Santa Cruz wanted to accept her successful book as her dissertation, but she felt that it wasn't fair to other students in her cohort. Instead she kept writing and revising her last work. *Light in the Dark/La Luz En Lo Oscuro* was just released in 2015, about eleven years after her death. Despite her ongoing battles with diabetes, she was still writing various pieces in several genres for a number of publications and lecturing while sharing many edited versions of texts with people she called her "writing comadres."

These are simply my observations, but the poetry of how Anzaldúa introduces terminology like autohistoria-teoría, borderlands, nepantla, Coyolxauhqui, nos/otros resonates more closely to my understanding of writing than any writing manual that I've pored over during all the years that I've pieced together when I try to convey what I do to other people. As a mixed race person who identifies as black, nepantla and the borderlands make sense to me as spaces I have constantly occupied. I feel most comfortable there. Certain groups will try to relegate me to the borderlands as margins or nepantla as the "middle space" where mixed people become tragic mulattos and misfits, and I've never considered myself any of those demeaning categories. The beauty of the borderlands lies in the beauty of exploring its permeability and flexibility, its subversive ability to transgress around and through the typical expectations and routes. We can safely say that Robert Frost knew little of this less-traveled road.

I also fully understand the power in Kate Rushin's "The Bridge Poem"—one of the poems that inspired by conveying an understanding of what women often do in this work (in *This Bridge Called My Back*) and in everyday life. The poem expresses Rushin's frustrations with connecting all these communities but never being able to focus on the self. A bridge is in a fixed position and everyone traverses over it. What allows us to connect to others and move? What gives us fluidity along the borders and in the subterraneous vessels that dwell in our skins and overlapping communities? It is not unusual that these growing connections evade the simple binary possibilities of Venn diagrams. A salad or a melting pot will not suffice either. If anything, identity strikes more like a quilt, a constructed entity with distinct qualities functioning as one continuous fabric, often held together by a backing that may rely on one particular material for its foundation, but even that comparison falls short. It is the idea of becoming una nepantlera, that moves, shifts, and travels back and forth, while remaining one's self, even if one dwells within and beneath the institutional frameworks that never acknowledge them, much like Fred Moten and Stefano Harney's idea of people operating in *The Undercommons*.

When Anzaldúa discussed inhabiting the Borderlands, I automatically understood that and gravitated toward her incorporating myths that were not Greek, European, and otherwise evading anything African and indigenous. I've also felt that Anzaldúa captured what it means to manage and negotiate the constant balancing of health, home, the precariousness of financial balancing, and continuing to write and establish relationships for the world you hope to see. I have told some of my students that we are writing for a world that is more conducive to our existence and our humanity.

> Life's whip makes welts and thin silver scars on our backs; our genetic code digs creases and tracks on our flesh. As our bodies interact with internal and external, real and virtual, past and present environments, people, and objects around us, we weave (tejemos), and are woven into, our identities. Identity, as consciously and unconsciously created, is always in process—self interacting with different communities and worlds...Identity is relational. Who and what we are depends on those surrounding us, a mix of our interactions with our alrededores/environments, with new and old narratives. Identity is multilayered, stretching in all directions, from past to present, vertically and horizontally, chronologically and spatially. (Anzaldúa 69)

Anzaldúa defining us as nos/otras, using the slash (la rajadura) to make one word into two more palabras, recalls Ntozake Shange's *for colored girls...* for me again, but it also speaks to how we are unified and multiple moving selves all at once, not just a fixed, essentialist idea. As a poet, that speaks to my entire existence. I move between different circles unnoticed, even though those circles are mine, sometimes to my benefit (and to my detriment at other times). Kyriarchy bends us this way and that when we consider how each of us is privileged, but if we are marginalized, it often happens on more than one front and almost always in a number of ways that compounds one stress upon on another, and people keep asking about mental illness, shorter life expectancies, and heart attacks. It's not just a colonized, processed diet or a lack of exercise in a shiny fitness center, it is the daily weight pressed against the sternum, the strumming throb of adrenalin flicked like a manic switch that contributes too.

> We are all strands of energy connected to each other in the web of existence. Our thoughts, feelings, experiences affect the others via this energy web. Our pervasive, excessive sense of woundedness compels to erect barriers that create knots on the web and block communication. When conflict (like a rock thrown into a web) disrupts a sense of connectedness, las nepantleras call on the "connectionist" or web-making faculty, one of the less structured thoughts, less rigid categorizations, and thinner boundaries that allows us to picture—via dreaming and artistic creativity—similarities instead of divisions. Las nepantleras develop esta facultad, a realm of consciousness reached only from an "attached" mode (rather than a distant, separate, unattached, mode) enabling us to weave a kinship entre todas las gentes y cosas. It removes hidden agendas driven by fear and ambition, is not invested in outcomes, and does not favor one view over another. Las nepantleras guard against reproducing exclusions based on racial and class identity. They see in surface phenomena the meaning of deeper realities, "see through" our own cultural conditioning and dysfunctional values. As agents of awakening (conocimiento), las nepantleras reveal how our cultures see reality and the world. (Anzaldúa 83)

In spite of the remolinos twisting us in the winds of conundrums, we can make realizations and joyful changes, or we can be amazed at our own resiliency. As I picture the fractured states of nepantla, I cannot help but think of "The Rose that Grew from Concrete," the famous poem by Tupac Shakur that countless young people have mentioned to me over the years. The most beautiful living beings do not need the nurturing of a hothouse to grow, and sometimes, they grow despite the resistance of seemingly impenetrable circumstances, and the beauty of it becomes all the more stunning. It brings me back to this rendering of a closed-eye Coyolxauhqui, butchered by her own brother, who awakens with eyes popping open as a startling illumination in the darkness, another concrete-like slab of desconocimientos.

Because women find a way to do this in a world that consistently devalues being human, being a woman, being brown, and being alive. Because tejemos, because of this "web of connections," and because my personal fascination with spiders led me to discover that the spirit animal or totem meanings for arachnids have always been that of creation and writing. Even though the Christian overtones of "a stone falling through a web" recall Edwards' "Sinners in the Hands of An Angry God," spiders know that conflict can rend what has been built, but it also makes space for the web to be built in less vulnerable places. Anzaldúa makes me consider how to make the writing stronger, a writing that can withstand multiple fronts, and exist in unlikely places.

WORK CITED

Anzaldúa, Gloria. *Light in the Dark/Luz En Lo Oscuro: Rewriting Identity, Spirituality, Reality.* Ed. AnaLouise Keating. Durham: Duke UP, 2015. Print.

One-Off

José Antonio Rodríguez

The time's running out and the list I and the couple of participants have put together on the chalkboard of the different roles/subjectivities we inhabit in our everyday lives reads like the self parsing itself out: student, friend, son/daughter, male/female/intersexed, romantic other, citizen/alien, gay/straight .... No one in this room inhabits all these roles but each of us certainly inhabits many, I say, hoping we can take a moment to appreciate the vast complexity of our lives. And I wonder about the cultural particularities of life here in a working-class wing of the city of Atlanta, of visiting this university in which I conduct a poetry workshop.

Hoping to rein in their focus and attention, I ask them to take a few minutes to jot down three roles they feel are particularly significant for them or hold special meaning. What roles do they most fear, do they most treasure, do they most fully inhabit? They scribble on their spiral notebooks. My eyes rest on the worn down desks, the flesh-colored plaster walls, and I am comforted by the absence of modern technology inside this classroom. Here, today, it is a relief.

We share some of the roles we've jotted down. I share mine in no specific order: immigrant, son, student. Now, I say, take a few minutes to recall an experience that challenged, dismantled, or revealed one of these subjectivities.

The plan was to have them write a poem that began at one moment in this experience, offering the participants a strong starting point that could prove generative and inspiring. A starting point that might serve to illustrate the important truth that our lives can be the stuff of poetry too—because after several years of living creative writing in the classroom, I've heard too many students who don't yet believe it—but I've run out of time. As a relatively young writer, I'm not always successful in framing these one-off workshops within the allotted time, and this irks me. In any case, I tell them as much and offer them this prompt as homework. At this precise moment I am reminded of a workshop led by Mark Doty that I attended a few years ago, where he also gave us homework, and it tickles me. I don't feel so bad then, assigning homework.

As I'm wrapping up, puzzled briefly by the chalk on my hands—chalk that always smells of elementary school—one of the participants, a high school student, raises her hand.

But what poets do we read? she asks.

Having stressed earlier the importance of reading to the development of a writer, I sense only now the overwhelming implications of that statement, the enormity and amorphousness of the endeavor. I'm stuck. What DOES she read? Who? In what order? Where? What has she already read? After a few uhh's, I tell her a good beginners' poetry craft book with plenty of sample poems to illustrate themes and exercises, such as *The Poet's Companion*, may be a good place to start. Then I trickle out a few contemporary poets whose work I admire and recommend: Terrance Hayes, Naomi Shihab Nye, Mark Doty, Joe Weil. Marie Howe, I think but don't say. But I draw a blank after that brief list. If you enjoy a poet's work, I tell her, go to the book's acknowledgments page to see what journals have published them and visit the journals' websites, try and get your hands on an issue. It's a start, I think. And before I know it, the workshop ends and I'm gone and sitting at the airport gate waiting for my flight out and back to south Texas.

Gloria Anzaldúa, I think, when I search for other poets I could have suggested. Then I realize that if I had to pick one poet to call my biggest influence, the one whose poetry I am most grateful to have come across, I would pick her.

Years ago I was a struggling master's student in the English department at The University of Texas-Pan American—stumbling, scrambling, scribbling erratic attempts at poetry, afraid to speak the thing directly because it eluded me and I eluded it. The course was Mexican-American Literature and the reading assignment was *Borderlands: La Frontera*, a truly hybrid text, a trailblazer in redefining genre—a combination of cultural criticism, spiritual treatise, auto-biography, ethnography, poetry. When I finished reading it, my first thought was, "Where has this been all my life?" Then I lamented the years lived without Anzaldúa's beautiful words.

Influence, as I have heard it expressed, is often calculated by style. Whose poetry has been instrumental to the ways you construct your poems? In my case, though, Anzaldúa's influence is most significantly measured in content, themes, subject matter, tone. She was the first poet I came across who wrote about the concrete things I knew and wrote them with a mixture of sorrow, anger, and joy. Don't get me wrong, it wasn't that I hadn't appreciated poetry before hers. I certainly enjoyed the imagery, rhythms, and cadences of Robert Frost, of Walt Whitman, of Emily Dickinson, but the worlds they created on the page never felt immediate and when they wrote "we," I never really felt included. This is often part of the minority experience when confronting literature of the American canon. It was some other "we" that they were invoking, *those* Americans whom they referred to and whom they called their own, Americans whom I couldn't help but see as white and wealthy and distant.

My home in the town of McAllen, an overwhelmingly brown town located in a far corner of Texas, a far corner of the United States entire, didn't feel like it belonged in poetry. After so much reading of snow in poetry and prose, it never occurs to you that literature could be set anywhere that doesn't snow, ever, like south Texas. But Anzaldúa wrote about arid lands, about nopales, about the sweltering heat of migrant field work, about cabbage crops, about brown-eyed anguish and blue-eyed power. And she wrote about the painfully magical place called the border—that bridge, that river—la frontera, where belonging and unbelonging was always a negotiation. Is always a negotiation. She said it: I may be everything the center calls me, the embodiment of the margins, but I will claim this space as my own and from it carve a new consciousness pregnant with conflict, beauty, silence, and song. As an immigrant poet, as a brown poet, as a Spanish-speaking poet, as a poor poet, as a queer poet, I felt found by her words. My poems flowed then. The vast majority of them poorly crafted, much too literal, not enough compression of meaning, but they were the best beginning, nonetheless—a beginning of release, of permission, of voice. The good stuff would come later. The best stuff, I'm thrilled to know, is still ahead of me. But there she was at the beginning. Simply put, she gave me license.

As the plane returning me home accelerates on the runway, the weight of the mechanism bearing down the second before it leaves the ground, I know if I had to pick an identity or subjectivity and an experience that revealed it, the poem would be about becoming a writer that day when I finished reading Anzaldúa's book. That day would be the moment.

The airplane levels off, I take out my journal, I see the students at their desks, their inquisitive eyes, their eager pens, and I hope that they find the moments, or rather that the moments—the ones that destroy and create, that support and redefine, that challenge and reveal—find their way to words.

Un Grito for GEA[1]

David Hatfield Sparks

At the center of a certain universe, where Golden Gate fog meets urban hills, outcrops of jagged rocks materialize fist-like across the crystal sky—symbols of resistance and revelation in a long sought place of shelter and defense. Shaken by winds, both pacific and ill, grow fragrant pines, eucalyptus trees, and feathery pampas grass. A camp's stone circle, with fire and incense, becomes like a sacred shrine to lost god/desses. Here, at the heart of San Francisco, high above the Castro at Market Street, we climb on terracotta red rock bringing corn and grain, tokens and trinkets, offerings to invoke the ancient gods of Lammas. Take our many sacrifices, inspire our bent genius; Many-Skilled One, may we harvest our victories with our ripened dreams.

At this natural crossroads of earth, sea, and sky, of bodies, minds, and wings, like monks gone astray after prayers, we say farewells to the dry husk of our closeted, false selves and contemplate our new raiment of drag angels, naughty novices, and pagan sprites, then descend back into the mundane chores and ecstatic rites of queer ghetto life below. But here and now, faithful to disco queen Sylvester's command to "be real,"[2] we are living openly queer lives encountering revelations and reprobation, precious Woolf-esque "moments of being" rarified and subterranean, here outrageously open and public; here extraordinary moments mesh with the fragile stuff of everyday life.

Singing Oz songs and *corridos* with abandon to our hilltop writer's co-op, we climb up Castro Street hill, high above our queer ghetto, high on brownies from Browny Mary, disco dancing towards the high camp and deepest song endeavors, dressed in Hallowmas drag, you as Sekhmet (Chicana-Liz Taylor-style), me as a Blue Star Night Dancer, Randy as chiffon clad Liza, with a Z, in this lived dream, "Nella Fantasia,"[3] as pop opera divas sing, we see a more just world, El Mundo Zurdo, forerunner of a 6th Sun, a queer Underworld exposed

---

1   *A Shout/Song for Gloria Evangelina Anzaldúa* (I called her GEA for short as a reference to the goddess Gaia, but queer, as in Gay-ya). This prose-poem is excerpted from an unpublished spiritual memoir entitled, "Wings of Eros." This piece is also dedicated to my partner/husband of 36 years (two years legal) Randy Conner and our daughter Mariah and her husband Prado.

2   "Realness," a term from song lyrics of SF Black drag star, disco singer Sylvester, that we turned into a borderland's, neo-cultural, and theoretical term for an aspect of queer "being and becoming," or in Gloria's *lengua*—queer *mestizaje*.

3   "Nella fantasia," is an Italian popular song by Ennio Morricone, Italian lyrics: Ferraú. See at: http://lyricstranslate.com/en/nella-fantasia-my-fantasy.html#ixzz3wbDigNlr

by art, by poetry, by song queerly, manifesting our humanity from the depths of our souls.

A place where body/mind/soul are free, complex, and boundless, flitting from life to life, from border to border, between worlds, on this unending illuminated night of Samhain, the *Día de los Muertos*, when the veils between worlds, between souls, barriers between races and genders are radically torn apart. We reclaim this Sodom by the sea. From this in-between place we root out, dig for hidden histories, archaeological omissions, write apocryphal texts for a revolutionary Aztlán-Atlantean new age.

When you hear this deep song that we sang with castanets, wearing black lace, flamenco heels, stamping our newly discovered pulse in this deep night, or walking into some twilight, some orange sunset, some blood red moon, less like some Hollywood movie, than a rending of clothes, a wailing of mourners, do you wonder, "Did our *cantos jondos* blossom from Lorca's tightly squeezed bud into a thousand petalled lotus? Or are we Lot's wife leaving Sodom behind, looking back too soon, turning into pillars of salt?" We the queer exiles, disowned by family, by race, by religion, we become new family, of all races.

It's hard to see through the still raw nerves, even after years, when I feel you lie, not as Pacific ashes floating towards forgotten isles, but, not respecting your wishes, in a grave under that hated South Texas sun, lying in your *charro/a* bride black suit, sparkling with *botonería* buttons and braids. Ay! I cry like Lorca, accompanied by a blue guitar, awakened from a shallow sleep, wailing, shaking, sweating. We hear the rooster's fatal song at dawn, *la paloma's* mourning at dusk.

At the center of another mundo, un poco picante y mas profundo, one centered at 24th and Mission Street, I found in exile, a new home—in living color. In another Oz ghetto, edged by the Castro, South of Market, the solid stone omphalos of Bernal Heights, and the baby strollers of Noe Valley. It's 1978. I'm working in the heart of San Francisco's Latino district. Cal-Mex spanglish gets me by in the neighborhood.

Twenty-fourth Street, heart of the Mission, is tree- and shop-lined, with galleries of local art, family-owned restaurants, panaderías, Discolandia blaring exitos, and botanicas—religious shops with statues of Catholic saints and African deities, full of herbs for healing, santos' candles in glass for novenas, and with more kitschy, gory crucifixes than I have ever encountered before. Like my early rearing, and yours in rural America, death is never far from life. It is accepted and ancestors fed pan de muertos and sugar cream pie.

Working in a local coffee house, La Bohème, I'm sent to buy fresh tortillas and Italian pastries from nearby bakeries to resell, and avocadoes to brighten salads and sandwiches. For breakfast I get myself two *cocos*, Mexican macaroons, to have with my first espresso of the day. Before opening the café at six a.m., I bask momentarily in the sunny street, a benefit of living in this niche protected from the city's daily summer fog. From this enclave, I hear the mixed tones of the old Salvadoran men playing "bones" on mismatched oak tables, the lilting chant of the *santera* across the alley, the din of socialist speakers and fundamentalist Christians hawking their pamphlets at the BART subway entrance across the street, buzzing by a gaggle of drag queens are returning home, like the Grimm's seven sisters, from a night of dancing with frogs and princes. You order a chai latte, and at my breaks we talk poetry, land, politics; this is how the personal becomes the political, becomes the spiritual.

Between the rush hour push of straight Black, Latino, Anglo workers, I catch the glimpse of the dimpled cheeks of a rumpled leather queen in chaps straggling behind. Into this somewhat tawdry, baroque, if operatic scene insert yours truly, a struggling queer artist with a five-year-old daughter. That our family of two might cause horror to some hardly ever enters my mind; only the rightness of the situation and a dedication to rearing my daughter govern my waking hours. My life finally seems to mirror my childhood vision of a world in which all races—and now also classes, genders, sexualities—beautifully, harmoniously comes together. A queer *mestizaje* out of the mouth of *un chulo blanco*.

KENNST DU DAS LAND? SABES TÚ LA TIERRA?

At the center of this patchwork vision, in lucid dreams, I am driving along a maze of country roads, a flat landscape like the Midwest corn fields of my roots in another farmland of the Mississippi/Ohio/Wabash river basins from which I am exiled. Many times this trip led us along a charmed path along the Pacific coastal highway from Oz to Santa Cruz, crazy wizards to holy crosses. Here and now, near your Mexican Gulf hot winds oppress, a mal aire keeps us off center, off course. En tú valle there is corn, but the landscape is más tropical. Enormous palm trees dot the horizon, with aloe vera and prickly pear, ripe for picking from life-blooming cacti. But it's not a lark or dream, but a waking nightmare as our flagged procession eerily floats along towards empty roads, the isolated cemetery near Hargill, Texas to bury you.

Your Tex-Mex recipes and Conjunto rhythms didn't come fully alive for me until our Randy brought me home to Tejas, to Austin, to San Antonio where the border really begins. Then your *masa* for tortillas, *nopales* de-thorned for eggs, for *chile Colorado, muchas cosas para fuego* began to mix, to fuse with my rural childhood's sweetened corn bread, hominy, and hoe cakes to create another bond between us; once fenced in by acres and acres of corn or cotton, their silks, filaments, and balls floating dusty and mysterious, transitory yet eternal.

These family fields and multigenerational homes and communities were probably the most valuable thing our families possessed and have lost; yours to migrant fields, mine to stark factories, day laborers, and shop girls. Corn is nature's bond we share; our other, labeled "unnatural." It was *korn* to my father's people, *maiz* for yours, an icon of seasonal passage in our mutual borderlands between the Rio Grande and the ancient Great Lakes. Corn should be knee-high by July, ready to eat by August, the harvest for survival, the fields cleared and stalks bundled by Halloween, their dry rattle, the voice of the dead. Then slash and burn the fields as sacrifice for renewal; we make corn dollies for play, corn husk masks for midwinter to honor the plant's rebirth, remembering the divine revelations of nature.[4]

Husking and boiling, the sweet buttery juice dripping down our faces from cobs devoured. From you I learn to spice mine with *chile*. Corn/Korn, the reds, golden browns, the yellow oranges, and the blues, the "Indian" corn, Indiana and Mexico, miraculously still rooted in the ancient foodways carried forward and adapted by waves of *conquistadores* and immigrants cross-fertilizing, grinding into purpose, now becoming queer corn,. You say, "*somos el mocajete*, the mixed portion."[5] We are the hidden crop, yet another sacrificial "drop of blood," refertilizing all life and sacred grain "into a single germ of life."[6]

WALKING THE LEFT-HANDED PATHS TO OTHER WORLDS

Zurdo, Surdo del sur—los que usa la mano izquierda, southpaw, a direction less taken, path less trod, forking path, magical path to multidimensional worlds manifest, toward the direction of fire. That which is contrary to the right-handed way of writing, of making, of being. The essence of that which is from the south, across rivers, across consciousness, the origins of civilization silenced, misterioso, estraña, and queer. From the ancestors, the First People's truths hidden destroyed in flames, in plunder, world illuminated, tongues aflame with hidden meanings, a flaming crown of el mística, zurcir-to darn, to mend, put together, think up, surcar—to plow, ready for planting renewing; surd beyond ordinary reason, wise fools dancing over realities ledges accompanied by carnival drums, el sur-do, played on the left side.

In the middle of our *mundo zurdo*, is a tree of life, a world tree, a tree that stands at the center of realities, the axis mundi mediating that which is above and that which is below, the Norse Yggdrasill, sacred oak of the Druids, Mayan Yaxche, Buddha's Bo tree of enlightenment, alchemical tree of the planets, Biblical Tree of Knowledge, and the Kabbalistic Tree of Life. One obscured central *sephiroth*, the energy center called Daat, becomes our entrance to the great Abyss, that in-between cosmic borderlands of transforming the self. With visions of god/desses and bodhisattvas, a more fluid definition self, not either/or, but both/and male/female/hetero/homo/bisexual, multi-colored, dark as containing all the wisdom universe, white as reflecting all color, a meta/physics, with all this we become *caminante* on the left-handed path, emptying out all the stereotypes and expectations before crossing the border of El Mundo Zurdo.

There, at the edge of the Pacific, queer *mestizo/a* crossroads meet abruptly at rainbow's end in a parade of carnivals, streaming protesters, prophets and tricksters conceding, finally, we all belong together, ground up together—

---

4   The Iroquois made corn masks worn during the rituals of the Husk Face Society. Fussell, Betty. *The Story of Corn*. Knopf: New York, 1992, p. 290.

5   Anzaldúa, Gloria. *Borderlands/La Frontera: The New Mestiza*. Spinsters/Aunt Lute: San Francisco, 1987, p. 81.

6   Fussell, Betty. *The Story of Corn*. Knopf: New York, 1992, p. 15, 31 and throughout.

somos el mocajete. Here our unions of loving twins can, our watering holes, be public, *al fresco.* We learn that our passion constitutes the same seeking of ideal love, a unique *mysterium coniunctionis*—not a sacred union of opposites, but a *monocolus*, the alchemical union of twins, contrasting sames, *el amor brujo.*[7] In this here and now, in between worlds, between sky and sea at land's end, or your fertile valley, my merging rivers, exists those earthly, metaphysical borders ... many more are awakening. A vortex where we might create new histories, new cultures. "By your true faces we will know you," you write in *Borderlands*, and that by becoming who we really are first "in our heads," we can then make it happen in the "real world."[8]

Xochiquetzal, sister, seated on your ocelot throne encircled by skulls, with marigolds, or cempoalxochitl ("twenty flowers"), we make offerings to the ancestors, abandoned, scorned, Guadalupe as Tonantzin, La Llorona, the lost god/desses. Protect us now and on the day of our death. We honor Xochipilli, flower prince in ecstasy, they who once ruled the Fourth, Black Flower Sun and are now returning. With spiders, weaving with the Norns, destiny's sisters, weaving the whole cloth of our lives, with words and tongues of fire burning, with the interrelatedness of life, we spin, we dance, we march to battle con Quenonas, with divine drag queens.[9]

With your sacred thorns, I pierce my ears, in honor of queer gods, as penance for losing you, for not loving you enough, for the sin of being a sissy, too feminine, or not being female enough, or masculine enough, for the sins imposed by another son crowned with thorns by an even crueler god. My heart weeps, weeps for us like a deer on his day of sacrifice, con los flores cascaduras, con los mundos enflamadas, fairies dancing in our heads, beds, defiant love, power, dreaming this dream—our vidas que son sueños.[10] *Now we weave together these bits and pieces, we reassemble the dismembered Coyolxauhqui, like putting Humpty-Dumpty back together again. Here is your son, covered with lilies, drugged with mushrooms and poetry, with your stone drums, I sound aloud the queer love I will always have for you, Gloria.*

---

7   A reference to Spanish composer Manuel de Falla's 1924 ballet of the same name.

8   Anzaldúa, Gloria. *Borderlands/La Frontera: The New Mestiza.* Spinsters/Aunt Lute: San Francisco, 1987, p. 86-87.

9   *Quenonas*—a Tex-Mex expression for drag queens, popular in the 1970s.

10   A reference to Pedro Calderon de la Barca's 1635 play, "La Vida es Sueño."

III

Dove

Barbara Jane Reyes

1. *Diwa*

before sound and dream   before speech   before our freedom was breached
before supply and demand   before this parceled, ancestral land   before strife
and fire, no light, no blight   before empire, no white flight   before warfare
rended us apart   before I split the lovers' bamboo hearth   before enforcing
my borders, torture orders, hoarding and whoring culture   before I was your
capital, collateral, damaged soul, I was liminal

2. *Amihan*

she flew between sea and sky, full wingspan wild   she lifted herself, the blue
above and beneath her roiling   she dove   she dove, and the light in her lungs
dimmed   she thought her heart would burst   she saw no resting place   she
weaved her body with wind   she called to sea, pushing through clouds   she
called to sky, throat forced utterance, utterance grown to word   and at her
command, the rocks flew from the hands of the sea   she saw rock and water
eddy and settle   she saw the islands they came to form   this is where my
father was born

this body

Miguel M. Morales

this body is geography
enfleshed, an historical marker of
the conqueror and the conquered.

this body is colonized,
constructed, and zoned by race, class,
gender, ability, and sex/uality.

this body is fluid
vital, flowing, surging, and eroding injustices
throughout the borderland and beyond.

this body is intersectional
chaotic, unstable, shifting, contradictory,
illuminating, and defying norms.

this body is textured,
stitched, and scarred. its woven fat, queer,
mestizo, fabric shimmers.

this body is epistemic.
this body is discursive.
this body is Borderland.

Things That Are Known about the Death of Roque Dalton, a Revolutionary Poet

Cecca Austin Ochoa

This is the face of Roque Dalton: Jar-headed, black hair like a cap. A thin, curved nose, one-quarter of a circle with elegant upturned nostrils. A feminine mouth puckered at the corners. And those ears. Trumpet ears, protruding like uneven parentheticals around the poet mind.

The revolutionary poet was killed by revolutionaries. The military tried to kill him, too. Once, he was thrown into prison and ordered to death by the dictator. The night before he was to stand, back to a wall, a firing squad lined up, aiming for fatality, the dictator was overthrown by a military coup. Roque was excused from his death that day. Lucky poet.

Roque wrote: "Everyday the dead are more restless."[1] The punch line is: The dead are becoming the majority. The joke is: the majority will overthrow the living. "*Antes era fácil con ellos: les dábamos un cuello duro una flor. Loábamos sus nombres en una larga lista.*" (Which is to say: "It used to be so easy with the dead, just give them a stiff collar, a flower. Praise their names on a long list.")

Let's talk about retrovision. You rolled your dice on triumphant futures. I looked back on that future and saw the no-hoper, the mass graves. Retrovision. Let's talk about revolution. I talk about revolution like it's a hobby:

The first time I slept with a girl, we were in the jungle. She had curly black hair that fell all the way down to the curve of her back. We were sleeping, not sleeping, in an abandoned house down the hill from K'inich Janaab' Pakal's tomb, the famous Mayan sarcophagus. She was traveling from Mexico City with her friends. They caught snakes and kept them in jars, they danced on tables in nightclubs for money, and made jewelry from bright colored thread and twisted wire. I fumbled into her orgasm, and she cried, *isn't this a revolutionary thing?* I tasted the bitter cream of her pussy in my mouth, and wanted a glass of water.

After the revolution, a memorial wall was erected in Parque Cuscatlán. Your name is there, Roque, carved into black stone, worn by fingers trailing over the letters. *There he is, the revolutionary poet! There he is, written on a monument, praised on a long list!* (Carved into the stone lid of the Mayan sarcophagus is a two-headed serpent that signals entrance to the land of the dead. (I wondered,

---

1   Lines in quotations are taken from Dalton's writing. Translation by author.

sticking my fingers into unknown dark holes, if I were close to the land, if the land of the dead could be found just beyond the flesh.))

Lo siento Roque, I am pampered in this new world. I am a queer in so many ways, and often, a coward. The way death scuttles in the corners of diaspora, I watch my feet, I prefer well-lit spaces. But sometimes, when I'm nosy, I open the drawers of my lover and peek in to find shame collected in lumpy piles. Maybe I slam the drawer disgusted. Maybe I pry further. Sneak into a door accidentally left unlocked and find a rape asphyxiated on the clothing rack. (Right next to that purple-striped shirt (the one that looks so bright on her.)) I shut the door quietly, so as not to wake the dead.

The military, furious at the revolutionary poet, sniffed him out, imprisoned him again, made him sit on his poetic hands and think about his execution. But an earthquake hit and cracked the wall of his cell. (Through which he dug a hole (through which he escaped.)) Lucky poet, the gods were watching you. He fled to Cuba, but knowing that he had to return home, for the revolution, underwent cosmetic surgery to change his face. Break that smooth one-quarter round of nose, pin back those trumpet ears.

Have you ever dated a transman before? He asked me, and I said "yes" even though I hadn't, because I heard: *Have you ever* fucked *a transman before?* Of course I had. There are incisions across his chest, down his arms, in other, secret, places. Plump and ropey, like earthworms. I finger the scars, without knowing how deep the wound goes. *What is it like to love me?* He asks. *Do you feel more like a girl? Do you feel less queer?*

It's like we're double agents, I say. *It's like we're undercover.* I hear treason, but see the two-headed serpent slither across the land and wonder, have I crossed over?

Roque, after your transformation at the hands of the Cubans (the revolutionary cosmetic surgeons) did you like your face? Did you stare into the mirror, and wonder where you'd gone to? Did you question the architect? Did you wish to escape the building? (Remember that time, they held you in prison, when the earthquake split the wall of your cell?) Did you ever look in the mirror for a crack to spoon the earth from? To emerge as you from? "*The window in your face/ sangre en la sangre.*"

The revolutionary poet was killed by revolutionaries. Some say it was a power struggle, revenge, a crime of passion. Some say that the Revolutionary Army mistook him for a spy, a double agent, a double-headed serpent that he (unrecognizable after his surgery) no longer wore the face of the revolutionary poet. Some say he was too powerful a revolutionary, too opinionated, too charismatic. That they recognized him despite the revolutionary cosmetic surgeons (probably because of his deep eyes (poet's eyes) unchanged by the knife). And so members of the Revolutionary Army were ordered to put him to death, and they either:

drugged him OR shot him in the back of the head (because they couldn't bear to look him in the eyes (his poet's eyes)). Some say the killer put a gun to his head, pulled the trigger, and said, "fucking poet."

Revolutionary perhaps has lost its meaning. Perhaps should only be taken in context. How do we measure the objective standards of revolutionary? What aesthetic do we apply? The fit, the misfit, the discomfit. I think there must be sadness, there must be sadness welling from an underground spring, wetting the emotional fauna. Even the long-stemmed anger, must be over-watered from sadness. The revolutionary taste, I think it must taste like gravel and blood, boot rubber and cracked leather. And the face, the revolutionary face, can be broken and reshaped, a disguise, a de-formation, but the eyes are always the same brown eyes. Sad eyes, barbed with anger.

I'm sorry if we've disappointed you (because I pass as a girl, (because I don't pass as a girl). Because I pass as a man, (because I don't pass as a man), because I am not a girl, because I am not a man). Because you are the revolutionary face. Because you are not the revolutionary face. I don't understand your face!
¿Te aceptas Roque Dalton? Do you accept yourself? The treasonous face of the revolutionary poet. Fucking poet. Maybe they just didn't like the look on your face.

Cenote Dreams, a 21st Century Utopian *Fábula*
Cordelia Barrera

In the beginning…

They whisper, *los ancianos.*
Somos los soñadores, y somos enojados para la vida.
　　Susurran.
And the people, glutted with fear and stained in war
Pour bones into the depths. Spill gold into the *norias.* Stream nightmares into the *río.*
Unquenchable Chaac. He wears red lipstick and plucks his eyebrows and they praise his masks.
And on *la frontera* the *río* quivers, expectant with biology.

AD 1514. El río is a vast delta called Great Waters. It runs swift and restless for two thousand miles, pulsing with minnows and shiners, chubs, and scuted shovelnose sturgeons. Tattooed *comecrudos*, lithe as new trees and dressed in shells, prowl the cattails and reeds of its southern banks to fish and feed off leopard frogs, red-eared sliders, spiny softshells, diamond-backed copperheads, the occasional blotched water snake, and all those tasty garters. To the north, wandering tribes of *cacalotes* make feasts of black water moccasins thick as cottonwood trunks.

AD 1770. The *Río Bravo* is Mother to a cascading water world whose center is a dance of a thousand circles of life. Fierce guardian of *cenotes,* primordial dreampools hot with memories of ancestral *Nahua* ways, these are days of plenty.

　　And the *río* winds into the people's dreams like a multicolored snake that pulses ancient ways and memories alive in their blood. As long as the *río* blazes wild, she nourishes sleepers with the old ways, powerful treasures of forgotten worlds.

AD 1994. La guerra marrón trae muerte. Título: Blood leads, *pesadillas* are Big News, and people don't choose their dreams.

There are white men with logos on their sleeves, *negro y blanco*, who cannot not see past the inconvenient black bubbles that rise to the surface of the *Río Grande* and *Pop! Pop! Pop!* like boiling blisters. The men have bled the river toxic and bankrupt, her nightmare stories glutted. The *titulares de pesadilla* blow over, snapped leaves dancing in wind.

A final sputter of bloated blue catfish and gray redhorses with their meaty lips, and *el río aperece desaparecer*. In its last days, the *Río Grande*—still called the *Río Bravo* by those who know her soul best—puts on a terrifying performance, what ancient *salineros* to the south once called a *jubileo*, a terrific die-off that lives in the tribe's bones for weeks, a spectacle of the senses. For too long, the *Río Bravo*, her brown waters the color of tepid *café con leche* has been pushed to the realm of night and *titulares de pesadilla*, an open wound for *los atravesados*. For too long, the people have dreamed of waters not brown—oceans and rivers like the Pacific or the Mississippi—blue, white-capped deeps that New York book publishers communicate in black and white ink.

When nightmares conquer dreams—the dreams of a *río* that is really a multi-colored *serpiente*—the visions cease to flow. Just like the *río* itself. No one—not the squint-eyed, the queer, the troublesome, the half-breed, or the half dead are afforded the painful luxury to even dream of a wasted and dammed dumping ground that has become a toxic trickle of smoldering ooze in some places.

Penetrable as stone in the age of machines and men, Great Waters, *El Río Bravo* is caught, bound, drowned.

And the *Río Bravo parece robado* and the *serpiente* seems vanquished.

And yet...

for the people who live in the little barrio—not all of them, but some—*el río's cenotes* yet whisper in little itches that tease their insides.

Susurran.

And when the white men with the *insignias negro y azul* on their coats abandon the *río*, the barrio people are again free to flock to her troubled drizzles and pools. To pay their respects, to remember. Sometimes the ones with *la facultad*, the ones who hunger most desperately, catch glimpses and snatches of little wormy tendrils of life. When they look closely, some imagine they see tiny snakes, *serpientes minúsculos* all aglow and writhing to life in the oily ooze that was once the *Río Bravo*.

Somos los soñadores, y somos enojados para la vida.

Susurran.

AD 2055. Recuperación. And years later, when the Earth is so much concrete and ash, she comes, *pura indita.* The quickening serpent movement with eagle eyes. *La chica serpiente* to carve the old bones anew and amplify Their whispers.

Somos los soñadores, y somos enojados para la vida.
    Susurran.

Delivered of need within the womb of the Earth Serpent, *la chicanita jota* defies the conquered spaces. *Pura musa,* she comes. When the *río* has not quite disappeared from the people's dreams, she prods the old memories from *los intersticios.* She comes first to the ones who are *Nahua* descendants and whose barrio has cradled the *río* for generations.
    But others will follow.
    And with her wild tongue she forks through shame. And with primordial ink, Red and Black, she recovers the names: *Tonantsi, Coatlalopeuh, Coatlicue. Los Ancianos.*

In time
Their whispers will be heard.
    ¡Como *Gritos!*
And on *la frontera* the *río* quivers, pregnant with biology.

AD 2076. Indigenous Utopia.

    The *río* transitions.
    Becomes.
    And the serpent girl, *niña* of a lost valley
    Is a woman.
    Alien, *nepantlera, activista,* dyke.
    She is their Teacher.
        She is Our Leader.

And the *río* pulses.

Becomes a cloud, flailed dust in a windstorm, multitudinous dreams of possibility impossible to snag. Now is the *río's* Becoming Time, a time of biology and devolution, so unlike the movements of men's clocks. The ancient *río se ha despertado.* She is a time zone all her own and much older than humankind. In this time zone animals talk, waters roar, and people listen. *Los ancianos gritan.*

And the *río* teems.

Like a corpse flower in full bloom and enfolded in mythic time, *el Río Bravo canta,* her *cenotes* boiling, satiated and screaming ancient ways and visionary ways of knowing. *El Río Bravo,* gorged now on the light of myth, is Our expectant Mother.

Her contractions begin. And the Earth's course changes. And the people, beautiful and brown, sing.

> And *la chica serpiente's* journey is that which abides.
> And her journey is ours.
> And now
> We blink in the night with a thousand sleepless serpent eyes. As one.
> > *Completa.*

We Are Not Afraid.

Follow Me Down, Down, Down (Under Skin so Brown)

Oswaldo Vargas

I have been in a hole for the past week.
  And it might be the deepest hole yet?
    This tastes different, I think, *I'm in the throes of something else.*
      A muscle sprain in my upper right thigh (which incidentally occurred as
        soon as I got up from the last meeting for this class)
          interactions with certain people
            and a disappointing grade
              has led to this.
And so I am in this hole,
  And very well might stay there.
    But a paradigm shift occurred—
      being "below" is not a bad thing.
        I saw Mama Cobb and Jesus Z. Moreno
          right after the seminar meeting on Monday,
            and Jesus spoke about seven directions instead
              of four: the four traditional ones, above,
                below, and the center, us.
Giving thanks to the ground below us,
  That was new to me in so many ways.
    That is why this journey is a staircase,
      the same one I descended (and still am)
        to meet the source of this state of funk I am in.
          I aimed to reach the center and speak to it.
            This is my *Conocimiento*, at its third stage,
              As outlined by Gloria Anzaldúa herself.
Jesus personally smudged folks
  so I lined up too but shuddered—
    will he see that I am in this hole?
      I was at my most tender; leg throbbing
        and heart and head racing for Calm.
          "Where from Michoacán are you from?"
            "From Los Reyes!" "LOS REYES? ÓRALE!"
              He had been there too. I haven't for
                twenty-three years and told him so.

And so he smudged to *Raizes*
    and how I must be in Michoacán
        in Head and Heart because as I
            and my branches grow so do
                the roots that anchor me to the earth.
                    My leg hurt like hell and a million thoughts
                        weighed me down but with the incense
                            and the hug he gave me after, I left
                                with tears of gratitude. On the walk
                                  back home I parted the earth
and marveled at the depths
    to which my *Raizes* went.
        But I also saw eyes!
            The Coatlicue state
                hit so close because it read like me,
                    failing my own self-placed expectations
                        (68 ON A DAMN PAPER). "I refuse to name
                            my demons" but I know how much teeth
                              they have. I want "Deliverance" but
                            I also "cling to my misery!"
                        Through the fissure
                      I went.

These eyes were not new—
    I knew them well, even
        as a queer brown seedling
            who worked farmland
                and dreamt of a knight
                    emerging from the corn
                      and escorting me through the stalks.
                        This was less than six months ago.
                          Behold, the first hole I left behind.
                          I am a climber who got good.

But even the best climbers
    have their days. Realizing
        that no corn knight will come
            and ICE can show up instead
                rattles your roots and downs the leaves.
                    In what might have been my darkest hour
                      a thing indeed emerged from the corner
                        and asked for my papers and when I'd
                          marry a woman. I chose not to tell it
                        about my marriage fantasy
                          to Prince Harry.

Do As Infinity's "Under the Moon"
    is a Japanese song that still
        gets down, down, down
            under my skin that is so brown.
                That is my "lunar landscape" incarnate
                    (currently trying to exorcise the demons
                        that hang from every one of its notes)
                            but I like to think I come down from
                                a long line of exorcists (my parents
                                  began my training very early
                                    y los agradezco).
I PERSEVERED AND WILL PERSEVERE AGAIN.
    Look how far we have gone down this staircase
        of mine, getting closer and closer to god-knows-what.
            But snaking along the staircase's railings are my ROOTS
                lightening my way down. My baptized mind figured
                    anything below = bad, but where else would
                        my *Raizes* be? The farther down I go the more
                            visible my roots become! I am heading for
                            the center, my center, one of seven
                            directions. Where competing
                            forces battle it out.
                                I can hear it.
This is the paradox:
    seeing your fears = ability to remove them!
        As I descend I weld my feelings into "tools
            or grist for my mill" on land that no one
            can colonize and mark for themselves.
                I can grow from what I see down here.
                    Like Gloria said, the stages are not
                      so orderly; all at once, one for
                          a month, one for years, who
                            knows? This hole of mine,
                              will I be in it for a
                              week or two
                                longer
                                ?
Will I get the grade I want?
    Will my temporary legal status
        be snatched? Will I have someone
            to call a better half? Will I get the job?
                Am I done with farm labor for good
                    or will it lull me back and have me
                        looking in between the corn stalks, hoping
                          for the knight again? As these questions yell

I shout "LOVE" at the heart of my
world, for past and future
selves to hear well.

I will climb out again,
with the comfort of knowing
my roots will keep my upright.
W.B. Yeats said the "Center cannot hold"
but that's because he never met me.
My center may shake but good luck
removing it from my calloused hands
that know a thing or two
about climbing.

IV

from Todavía El Valle es una herida abierta[1]
A 'transplant' in Aztlán (2015)
Emmy Pérez

Want to kiss the hands of our lover before moving elsewhere on the body[2] because the lover is the beloved, doesn't suddenly stop like a country.

Despite walls, rivers, checkpoints, drug-sniffing dogs

las américas don't suddenly stop—

The skin of the earth is seamless[3]

and the globe is round like toronjas plumping
on trees, like the bellies of billions
of pregnant women, each their own
cosmos, like eyes, our souls, with oceans,
with tides directed by the sun and moon's
gravitational pull

Kamala Platt's *These are our f'cking guns*[4] in Mexico is not a line of so-called "didactic" poetry to me. Studies prove that cussing relieves stress.

Sandra McPherson writes, to Elizabeth Bishop,
(but I use this for *each and her*)[5]

---

1 A few lines from this essay, some in different forms, were originally published in a 200 word essay as part of HL Hix's Progressive Poetics project: http://031454a.netsolhost.com/inquire/2015/04/25/emmy-perez/.

2 "Want to kiss the hands of our lover before moving elsewhere on the body" from my essay "Healing and the Poetic Line" in *A Broken Thing: Poets on the Line*, (University of Iowa Press, 2011), edited by Emily Rosko and Anton Vander Zee.

3 "The skin of the earth is seamless" from Gloria Anzaldúa's chapter "The Homeland, Aztlán: El Otro México" in *Borderlands/La Frontera: The New Mestiza* (Aunt Lute Books 1987).

4 "These are our f'cking guns" from Kamala Platt's poem "These are Ours" in *Weedslovers: Ten Years in the Shadow of Sept.* (Finishing Line Press 2014).

5 *Each and Her:* the title of Valerie Martínez's book (University of Arizona Press 2010).

I take the globe and roll it away: where
On it now is someone like you?[6]

They ride La Bestia's back—el tren de la muerte, el tren de los desconocidos—grip its metal fur, duck treetops, fall asleep, jump off, fall off.[7]

All the young women taking one-month birth control shots for the trek from Guatemala, Honduras, El Salvador, knowing what happens. All the women and children needing to walk, pee, sleep, eat under the watch of coyotes and polleros they paid. All the women and children surrendering to U.S. Border Patrol.

One spring dawn last year, a Border Patrol agent found three Honduran women—two of them teenagers—on the banks of the Rio Grande in Anzalduas Park (not named for Gloria Anzaldúa).[8] They didn't run. He kidnapped them, thought he left two for dead after raping and assaulting them outside, the third bound and assaulted in his home. When police and the FBI arrived, he shot himself.

A Guatemalan boy with an Elvis belt buckle and Angry Birds jeans was found a few months later, collapsed and exhausted forever, a mile after crossing the river, near La Joya in the monte, twenty miles from my home, still with the rosary beads his mother gave him when she begged him not to leave.[9]

Automatic machine guns sit mounted in armor-plated Texas Highway Patrol boats, Marine vessels with comfortable seats for DPS officers, drivers and boats creating literal waves as Mexican children swim in the afternoon heat on the Reynosa side of Anzalduas Park.

---

6   "I take the globe and roll it away…" from "For Elizabeth Bishop" by Sandra McPherson, Poetry Foundation website http://www.poetryfoundation.org/poems-and-poets/poems/detail/42853

7   When the numbers of migrants from Central America dramatically increased in 2014, Mexican officials took measures to discourage as many riders on the trains by speeding them up and including more border patrols and checkpoints.

8   Anzalduas County Park is on both sides of the border, likely making Anzalduas a plural word, spelled without an accent mark.

9   Nearly 50,000 unaccompanied minors were apprehended by border patrol in the Rio Grande Valley sector in 2014 and over 52,000 family units were apprehended: http://www.cbp.gov/newsroom/stats/southwest-border-unaccompanied-children/fy-2014

When tens of thousands of unaccompanied refugee children from Central America crossed into El Valle last year, then governor and presidential hopeful Rick Perry boosted his Operation Strong Safety campaign with a border surge of DPS officers sent to "combat criminal elements taking advantage of our porous border" and deployed 1,000 Texas National and State Guard troops to help "DPS's ongoing law enforcement surge."[10]

All the guns in the world at our border can't save refugees from deportation or detention or stop Americans from wanting and needing drugs.

In Eduardo Corral's "Border Triptych" poem for Gloria Anzaldúa, one woman sprinkles red gelatin powder in her underwear just before crossing the Tijuana/ US border, near our shared Pacific ocean, knowing that bandits await crossers, make them lower their pants:

I was one of ten women. Our mouths were taped.
I was spit on. I was slapped. The other women were raped.[11]

this "Tortilla Curtain" turning into el río Grande
flowing down to the flatlands
of the Magic Valley of South Texas
its mouth emptying into the gulf.[12]

This is la *herida abierta,* the *1,950 mile-long open wound.* On a map, El Valle seems to dip into Mexico, the tip of Tejas, la herida *dividing a pueblo,*[13] making the trek north for many a bit shorter. La herida abierta also has a mouth, a mouth that empties into the Gulf, la Boca Chica that will taste SpaceX, a rocket and spacecraft company whose "ultimate goal [is to enable] people to live on other planets."[14] Not a deportation scheme. The wealthy will blast off of this beach la migra patrols while elote/ice cream trucks continue to roll along the South Padre beaches just north of this one.

La herida abierta extends further north, beyond El Valle, into Brooks County's private ranchlands around the Falfurrias checkpoint, 70 miles north of the river,

---

10   Perry for President website: https://rickperry.org/major-border-action-taken-by-governor-perry

11   "Border Triptych" by Eduardo Corral, Web del Sol chapbook, Summer 2005. http://www. webdelsol.com/LITARTS/CORRAL/corralpoem2.htm

12   "This 'tortilla curtain'…" is from *Borderlands.*

13   "The U.S.-Mexico border es una herida abierta," "1,950 mile-long wound," and "dividing a pueblo" from *Borderlands.* I took the liberties of italicizing all of the text as a stylistic choice for this essay.

14   SpaceX website: http://www.spacex.com/about

where coyotes and polleros leave refugees to find their way through the brushland, the bodies and bones of many found later on, sometimes with a gallon of water beside them as if there finally comes a time when all bodily signals, ignored for weeks, shut off, to keep on, keep on, keep on.

The Falfurrias station first opened in 1940, the year of my Tejana mother's birth, two years before Anzaldúa's, and "remains the heaviest area of alien and narcotic traffic."[15]

Wound: *these are our fucking guns* and drugs.

Wound: that we roll through the Falfurrias checkpoint, from El Valle up to San Anto, in search of amusements we can't always find here: low sugar, whole wheat, lard-free pan dulce, indie films with pitchers of beer, live NBA basketball, writing workshops with famosa writers. Mostly, we pass through Falfurrias lines with relative ease, after a few annoying questions, mostly by raza, eyes entering car windows—once our English speaks.

A few years ago, when my brown, female self traveled alone: more delays, more questions.

Confession: As a child, I always wished my mother would buy me more under-clothes and maxi pads (tampons were not made an option) without me having to ask. I had one training bra through middle school and played sports daily. My mother's recent confession: growing up in Ysleta, Texas, they wore used underwear donated by her mother's friends. My father's: growing up in Brawley, California, his mom would make chones out of flour sacks emptied after dozens of daily tortillas de harina. Anzaldúa's confession: As a child, she'd take her bloody cloths "out into this shed, wash them out, and hang them really low on a cactus so nobody would see them."[16] Her poem "La vulva es una herida abierta" further describes the shame and pain of very early menses.

In her essay "The Homeland, Aztlán," *The U.S.-Mexico border es una herida abierta where the Third World grates against the first and bleeds. La frontera es una*

---

15   U.S. Customs and Border Protection website: http://www.cbp.gov/border-security/along-us-borders/border-patrol-sectors/rio-grande-valley-sector-texas/falfurrias-station

16   "Within the Crossroads: Lesbian/Feminist Spiritual Development: An Interview with Christine Weiland" from Interviews/Entrevistas: Gloria E. Anzaldúa (Routledge 2001), edited by AnaLouise Keating.

mujer—or is it the Third World that's mujer—because it's the Third World that bleeds before *the lifeblood of two worlds merg[e] to form a third country.*[17]

Last summer, when volunteers of Sacred Heart Church in McAllen sent out a list of items needed for refugee women and children: underwear and maxipads.

Grate as in shred. Grate as in rasp. One is a violent, physical transformation. The other an unpleasant sound, a noise. All genders bleed. The Third World is bleeding when it comes into bodily and vocal contact with us. And *the lifeblood of two worlds merg[e] to form a third country* here on the border, the country of a new, "unwelcome" culture in *los atravesados*, though the *lifeblood* implies survival, creation, hope. Meanwhile, *la mojada, la mujer indocumentada, is doubly threatened in this country* (the U.S.).[18]

Third world walks, rides, runs, swims to the first. Maybe reaching this *third country* of the border and its culture sounds like winning a bronze.

The first world here and beyond awards refugees with checkpoints beyond the river, deportation back to violence and poverty, long detentions, ankle tracking devices, and work few others dare touch.

Each person is a world and every one a first.

El Valle siempre es una herida abierta. New border walls between lactating mothers, over an hour waits in doctor offices, doctors that want to induce labor when no interventions are needed, and parteras don't advertise in coffee shop flyers. I am a transplant in Aztlán. White midwives and doulas, though not many of them, are easier to find.

At work, "El vato" greets me daily in the elevator. Someone had scratched out two letters from the word Elevator and immediately confirmed, during my job interview nearly a decade ago, this could be home away from home.

---

17 "The U.S.-Mexico border es una herida abierta" from Anzaldúa's *Borderlands*.

18 "La mojada, la mujer indocumentada, is doubly threatened in this country" from Anzaldúa's *Borderlands*.

Many young people del Valle rush to and from campus, work much more than other university students nationwide (like Anzaldúa), attend every family function, without hearing the thousands of footsteps of unaccompanied young crossers. There isn't enough time. Some undergraduate students in my courses say they don't watch the news because it is sad. Many hadn't heard of the 43 students of Ayotzinapa. I didn't read or watch the news much either when I was 20. Most are amazed, as I once was, that a Chicano poet and activist worked with Martin Luther King Jr., on the Poor People's Campaign. Martin Luther King, Jr., makes everything for real. This is the first time many have ever heard of a civil rights movement for their people. Most enroll in my introductory creative writing class simply to write poetry and fiction not knowing it is also a Mexican American Studies course. In 2015, about five in a class of 25 usually know Gloria Anzaldúa's name when I first ask, up from about three in 2006. I didn't know her name either when I was 20, but that was of different consequence.

Wound: many students had time to protest el Vaquero, our new university's mascot, because they are afraid *what will they think*, U.S. America that already thinks too much of us. UT Austin frat boys have parties in ponchos, sombreros, and construction gear.[19]

Wound: a few years ago, UT Pan American's Mexican American Studies Club members, endorsed by the Student Government Association, proposed to the faculty senate a diversity requirement, an inclusion course for the core curriculum, that was adamantly shot down by one vocal senator and then voted against by the senators. MASC member Gladys Ornelas reported, in her poem of witness written the same year:

las voces llenas de ilusiones
silenced
dismissed with his words,
"Your parents have failed you."

We entered unidos, con confianza
[…]

we were "American
not Mexican"
"slavery happened," he said
we need to "get over it."[20]

---

19 Members of LUCHA (La Unión de Chicanxs Hijxs de Aztlán), a student organization at UT Rio Grande Valley, have more recently protested the gendered language of Vaquero in the #soyvaquera campaign. UT Rio Grande Valley is a new university (Fall 2015) whose legacy institutions include UT Pan American and UT Brownsville.

20 "Open Letter to…," a poem of witness (currently unpublished) by Gladys Ornelas

Wound: student testimonios about the difficulty of coming out as lesbianas, trans women, or of returning home once out.

The LGBT student group at Pan Am is a victory, though a member tells me it is mostly comprised of men who identify as gay.[21]

Wound: all the relatively few remaining acres of monte with for sale signs— cactus blooming yellow roses, mesquites squat and green, sable-colored ébano pods scattered on the earth with seeds gone, spread. The death of snakes, the death of complexity, the birth of biggish houses squished together for the most profit for builders, and more big box stores and strip malls, the birth of bulldozed land planted with new seeds that will become tall trees after we are dead or our children have already grown, neighborhoods born as dust.

Wound: faculty encouraging new faculty to make sure they live "north of Nolana" St. in McAllen.

Wound: my colleague died from cancer a few weeks after a semester ended and had worked all semester long. To be working while dying in this country is yet another cruelty of capitalism.

Wound: being a "transplant" in Aztlán draws some Valley natives to you at conferences. Most you meet, or rather hear from in the Q&A, like Anzaldúa and like you from your Santa Ana, have made their lives away from their hometowns, las heridas abiertas. They size you up, your "authenticity," point out minor mistakes and "mistakes" in your representations. You don't wish to assume ownership of any earth, besides your own self. They are keepers of El Valle, carry las heridas with them wherever they now live and go. My whole family in California—my babies growing up without primas, abuelas, tías.

Keepers of El Valle, we walk with heridas abiertas too, and sometimes your quibbles feel like a contest in who can feel the most pain.

---

21   Shortly after this essay was written, I learned about and participated in the first Aquí Estamos Conference, "the first LGBTQ centered conference in the Rio Grande Valley," organized primarily by activists of all genders in their early 20's: https://aquiestamosrgv.wordpress.com/conference-2015/ . It was a great success, and continues to be, in its second year. Organizer Dani Marrero also recently compiled this list of "11 LGBTQ Organizations you should know in the Rio Grande Valley" http://www.danimarr.com/2016/04/11-lgbtq-organizations-know/

Dear Gloria,

If you were my mother, because you and my mother were both born at the same time, in the Tejas-Méjico borderlands, how different might my path have been? I probably wouldn't live in El Valle, or maybe I would? My mother's stories of her hometown Ysleta first moved me there and to the borderlands. If you had been my mother, of course you would have been my queer mother and spoken to me, I assume, equally in the languages you knew. I would have learned Chicana feminisms early on, though maybe I did learn some? Would I have learned sooner how to speak from shame and silence, how to avoid them from the beginning, and begin healing from the desconocimientos of colonization, sexism, and more. And yet, I do not blame my own mother or parents for my early pains. I measure and marvel at the perceived distances between you and she as a way to further understand.

And still, even with 15 years and counting here in Tejas, what does it mean to be a "transplant"? Except for four years on the East Coast in my early 20s, I have always lived in some part of Aztlán.

To have a heart transplant is to use someone else's heart because they are no longer living and have been generous enough to have the foresight to gift it to another. To be a transplant, if one must use it for me, is to be the whole plant, the whole body, treading the earth where we were not raised, though our own bodies too are worlds in and of themselves, sharing air, river, streets, botanas, poetry, pain. I, the whole plant, the whole person, who grew two children inside of my body and birthed them here, into El Valle, este mundo.

And this is where we live. Where I have chosen to live. And where we are alive.

Anzaldúa as Exile and Antidote to Fatal Simplicity

Dan Vera

I have to come to respect Gloria Anzaldúa's work as being deeply informed by her own experience of exile. And because of this I've experienced her work as a sort of spiritual and intellectual anti-venom to banality and simplified identity: a simplified identity that is false, does not serve anyone, and is dangerous.

On Anzaldúa as an exile—I mean the ways in which her work articulates a love of and longing for a home that resided inside of her. I mean to acknowledge her as a writer who spent much of her life away from the places she called home. As a writer who has spent most of my life living away from the places where I grew up, I feel that intimately. I believe the land resides inside of us and that as Pablo Neruda wrote, "If it dies in your blood you die out."

Perhaps my own thoughts are influenced by my own renewed sense of homeland. I recently had the opportunity to return to the Rio Grande Valley for readings. When my responsibilities were over, I spent a few extra days driving around the Valley. My parents, who came from Cuba in the early 1960s, settled in South Texas. So I relished the chance to find and visit the houses my family, my parents and grandparents lived in just a few miles away from Hargill, the town Gloria Anzaldúa grew up in and the town where she's buried.

Something about that pilgrimage through the small Valley towns of Weslaco, Mercedes, and Raymondville reinforced in me a deep sense of place. It began when I stepped out of the air-conditioned Brownsville airport and felt the air envelop me. That warm humid air of the Valley right after a rainstorm. And then in that moist air I heard a sound I hadn't heard in years. The sharp call of a bird I instantly recognized even if I didn't remember its name. I went kind of nuts at that moment. It's hard to describe being separated from a place for some thirty years and then all of a sudden hearing a sound that plucks some string inside of you and discovering the sound has lived inside of you all of those years.

> *Pardon me, if when I want to tell the story of my life*
> *it's the land I talk about.*   Neruda

> Every place has its names
> incantations of every place
> first encounter of memory

sound of memory
the color of sky
the voice in the trees
urraca
sound that lives in every tree
urraca
black call in sabal palm
cleaves through moist air
communicating itself
with every piercing cry

What do we have without the sound of the birds in the tree?

I depart for years then return
to discover the bird
that has lived in my chest
awaiting my return
memory is like this
no sound but *that* sound

Make a litany of the many names we call it
urraca, grackle, crow, cuervo
the myriad confusions that arise from not
paying attention to how a name is pronounced

Mispronounced—the bearer goes on
screaming her name from tree to tree

My time in the Valley had a planned itinerary itinerary and the last item was a visit to Anzaldúa's grave. Somewhere in the drive from Raymondville, the small town of my first memory, to Hargill, out in those open ranch lands, under that imperial blue sky, I felt so happy to be in such a familiar landscape.

I believe that Anzaldúa's work is inseparable from that land, that it sprang forth from that particular place on the planet to inform a sense of deep belonging. Her work wrestles with a given language, one that unifies without a true sense of diversity and she pushes against this false unifying to insist on a permeable language that would include *all* the forms that reside in a place—what comes and goes across borders.

When the border is invoked in the American imagination, the images are simplified to a John Wayne and saguaro cactus shorthand that cheats one of the most ecologically diverse zones on the hemisphere. It's in this simplifica- tion of flora and fauna that one sees the dominant worldviews of *us* and *them.* Experiencing the ecological diversity of the subtropical Valley, from chaparral to coastal shores, from great plains to Chihuahuan desert, one experiences the terrestrial roots of Anzaldúa's brilliant framework for identity—one that insists on a specificity of myriad truths.

This is the teaching of valuing the *place* you find yourself. Because in Anzaldúa's case we have a writer whose sense of place was also informed by a sense of exile from homeland. An exiled view that allows one not only a deep appreciation for the lost or the missed sense of tierra, but an acute appreciation for the beauty of what is right where you are.

What I love about Anzaldúa's work is its deep sense of integrity and a recognition of the uselessness of easy answers or simple identities. In Anzaldúa we have a writer who pushes us to those uneasy places of solidarity. Not liquidarity of the "Yay, we're all just the same" but the solidarity of "even through our differences we can find some deep places of resonances and shared connection."

I remember when I came across Anzaldúa's lines:

> To survive the Borderlands
> you must live *sin fronteras*
> be a crossroads.

I was mesmerized by this wisdom. To realize we are made up of so many borders we straddle and that this straddling is its own means of common humanity.

As I've had the opportunity to travel around the country I work to contemplate each place's beauty. In the world we live in that seeks to homogenize, that Velveeta-ization that our cities and towns are becoming more and more, we need to recognize the ground underneath. We need to sound out the many names of place and many names of the birds and the trees and the flowers of a place. These names are not soft power, they are hard power because they become an incantation of place that strips away the false layer, because we are naming the surviving living emblems of belonging.

And in naming the names we bring these things to life. We "make mantra of American language" as Allen Ginsberg counseled in his anti-war poem "Wichita Vortex Sutra." In the Vedic tradition a mantra is not only the name of the deity, Shiva, Ganesh, Kali, but the breath from the lungs in forming in the space of the mouth, the position of the tongue as the breath is forced out of the mouth, all these positions, in that space the deity is not only invoked but is present. Which is to say the symbol *is* the sacred present. The words matter. The words are the way in which the world comes to life.

So many of us—if we are still for a minute—can recall the place we grew up in... hear the sound of the birds in the trees...the distinctive place.

If you live far away from the place of your first song and first breath, you come to realize that you are floating inside a different breath and hearing a different song every day of your life. You are caught in an act of perpetual translation. Very similar to the experience of being bilingual, that is a fluency that allows you to inhabit two languages at the very same time. Or as Anzaldúa wrote

> because I am in all cultures at the same time.
> *alma entre dos mundos, tres, cuatro,*
> *me zumba la cabeza con lo contradictorio.*

But the key is to remember that we are all doing this at the very same time. And wherever we find ourselves, in the different places on this earth we share, they *all* resonate with whispers of that first place. And in acknowledging this we come to understand that just as there is no one border, there is no one world. And that we want, as the Zapatista saying goes,

> un mundo donde quepan muchos mundos. [We want a world in which many worlds exist.]

In order to achieve this, we have to wrestle with what it means to live without borders, to live without internal borders of meaning and knowledge. I believe we know this innately but we live in a culture that adores the simplicity of either/or and demands it from us, constantly seeks to have us choose sides and singular identities. It is this simplification that endangers us all. It's the way that terrains are simplified, how diverse multicultures of species are made mono-cultures of agriculture. It's the way humanity is processed through an infernal mechanism filled with bleach, where diversities of people and languages and histories are rendered white and black, a dualistic framework that legitimizes white supremacy on the basis of an artificial binary that leads us to nothing but continued misery.

Our task is to render the either/or obsolete, to reject the false simple and to reveal it as inadequate cover for our souls. Our work is to recover and honor the incantations of names, the specific ways we have known home and land and sky, blood and bone and breath: these are the ways we move toward a future of balance and honesty. It is about moving beyond either/or to both/and. If we don't, we are lost in oblivion.

Oblivion believes Democracy is untranslatable
Oblivion believes our fathers were incapable
of understanding the ballot
were unworthy.

Believes Democracy, like Jesus, only speaks English
Believes fluency in English
is the requirement for the franchise.

In college Oblivion minored in your native tongue
wants to argue the proper usage of the subjunctive clause
of the language of your first lullaby, your early dreaming.

Oblivion wants to argue grammar and syntax of your speech.

Oblivion once stayed in a tourist zone in your home country
became an expert on its over 500 years of history
forgets to mention the 12 times his great grandparents visited in uniform
Oblivion has never been good at history.
Now comments on the current conditions of its inhabitants and its refugees.

Oblivion wakes you up at four in the morning holding a pad and pencil
wants you to tell him what you've been dreaming
through decades of cultural displacement.

Oblivion just got here and already knows all the changes
that have to be made.

Oblivion walks after young black men in Florida
forgets the songs his mother lulled him to sleep in Spanish,
clings to his pistol and his patriotism.

Oblivion is running for president
as God's appointed candidate
for border walls and the evils of Muslim terrorists
pontificates on purity to a crowd that would
have strung up his father when he bribed
his way into the country.

Oblivion declares she sees no color only white and black
if pressed, Oblivion will make room for other people
for a few minutes, on special days and months,

Oblivion would like you to join his club.
But won't tell you the rules or the price of admission.

Oblivion once spoke with an accent.
Oblivion once wore his ethnic dress.
Oblivion read the local paper in his native language
celebrated strange lunar festivals in the old neighborhood.

Oblivion's great granddaughter was just elected to the Senate
she smiles widely before the cheering crowd
and proudly tells reporters she authored legislation
denying the vote to people who don't speak the language
her grandfather sacrificed the language of his dreams to.

Oblivion's granddaughter still bears his name
pronounces it in ways he never would have recognized.

Oblivion, I am speaking to you.
Oblivion, when did you lose your name?
Who took it from your grandfather hands?
Oblivion, I declare to you, I did not rise up to fall inside of your emptiness,
your plastic canyons, your staggering forgetfulness.

Oblivion, I want you to wake you
demand that you recall your own name
show you your face in the mirror
the creases of history around your eyes
the curling lip of bitterness
your supremacist sneer.

Oblivion
I want to tell you to pull off the layers of pancake and blackface
I want to remind you of everything you've lost
to coax from your tongue, the place names you mutter in your dreams
to rend your dress of acceptance
your coat with its shiny medals.

There is more to you
than what ever you cling to in your fear.

Oblivion your imaginary past
was never a home for you
the future of honesty is the only
chance you have
to be real and free.

THE EXILE

Michael Wasson

Chilocco Indian School, Oklahoma, 1922: A disciplinarian says, *There is no foolishness, do everything just so...such as keep your room clean, keep yourself clean, and no speaking of your Native language.*

For now I can
        just whisper
kál'a sáw

           the *'óxoxox*
    of your *hím' k'up'íp*

wrecked at the base
          of a century that burns

through my slow blood

    i.

        kiké't caught

in the blink   *silúupe*

so draw the eyelids
      shut & forget the fire
tangled among the branches

of your spine
      start where the skin meets

half an autumn
      rusting the edge of winter that is

knifing   between me & *'iin*

you & *'iim 'ee*

i.

boy   have you forgotten us

                                         is not what they are saying

or are they   asks another century

               how are we remembered
     in our choreography
of bones?

i.

mouth your birthplace   boy
without mouthing off   *tim'néepe*   is *at the heart*

or *the heart of the monster*

               or *the grass blood-soaked*

from the fresh kill that finally isn't

               your father

& pray *héwlekce* when your body is given away   says the orphan boy

         with lashes licked into his shoulders

forget *'im'íic*   because they can   tear every lip from every memory

         of your mother

i.

because you are
torn & because you are
what song fills
    your throat
with the color
    of carved out tongue

peewsnúut & *hi'lakáa'awksa*
       is what is voiced in the dark
& so what does it mean
       asks the boy

    i.

as the moon
glows mouth open
to the unbearable
taste of ash
blown among the stars

that the boy learned
the ghost's trail

that *milky way*
is lit by the dying
brightly echoed

    i.

c'ewc'éewnim 'iskit
so there had to be breathing

there had to be.

Eclipse in Morristown

Melanie Márquez Adams

Hidden in a remote nest of tiny blue hills
a town beats alive to the sound of two hearts.
They live side by side, yet thousands of shades apart.

Howdy Morristown!
Why do you look away?
Can't you see your dark-skinned neighbors
sharing next to you the faithful shade of the maple tree?

Quihúbole Morristown?
Don't let your gaze drop down.
Why do you walk the other way?
You are not mischievous squirrels.
They are not feisty dogs

Show them your proud eyes!
They won't hurt you. They won't bite you.
They don't know what to make of you
just like you don't know what to make of them.

Floating around and between these two worlds
a wild transgressor, a hummingbird feeding from both sides.
My undefined-colored-wings flap here and there,
crossing the invisible lines.

¿De dónde eres? ¿Qué eres?
Are you Mexican, are you Asian?

The good Christian folks squint...
she is not completely dark but yet
a shade we can't classify.

La gente from the other side wonder as well...
her eyes and hair look like ours,
but yet something is not quite right.

My ambiguity exonerates me.
I am allowed to play on both sides
yet I cannot belong to either.

I witness two cities in a city repel each other,
suspended in time sharing an absurd motionless stage.

The saturated smell of funnel cakes and grits
yearns to join the spell of fresh cilantro and peppers.
Corn dogs here! ¡Corn tortillas más allá!
No cross overs allowed.

A piñata swings waiting for the final blow
winking at the bean bags aimed at the holes.
A soccer ball and a Frisbee meet in mid air
so close...longing to touch...
Warm music ripples to the rhythm of the summer rain
bouncing in a mirror of gloomy disdain.

I zigzag through plantains and squashes,
bluegrass and boleros, Selena and Carrie.
I wish to melt in both worlds but alas,
I drift aimlessly
trapped in a game of la bola que rebota
over and over again.

If I could come up with a word that meant both Órale and Hell Yeah
maybe then… the bouncing would end.
The barriers coming down with the thunderous storm,
both worlds sharing a space in a brief eclipse.

The blowing grass smells of dumplings and tamales,
fat pitchers brim with horchata and sweet tea.
The banjo and la trompeta fall in love,
tempting the swaying crowd to succumb to the long-awaited affair.

I dance with tipsy clogs and a bubbly sweeping skirt.
I dance until my tanned cheeks burst of giggly red.
Shining through the eclipse and joining the crowd
I curtsy
To the mountains, to the sun, and to mi querida Morristown.

What's the Brown Part of You

Tomas Moniz

1.

The first time my father held me, arms chubby and legs fat like little sausages, he poked at me and said, "This one's a Chiconky." It was just like my father to mash two things together into a new thing: Chicano, Honky. Years later, he'd ask me like a dare, "What's the brown part of you?" When angry he'd growl, "That's the white part of you." When high or desperate or lonely, he'd whisper, "I love every part of you." Legacy is a thing passed on and a thing remembered. It's a tension. Because of my father, I learned to fret about the parts, piecing this to that, sorting out what belongs and what doesn't. But he also taught me to recognize that shit don't always make sense, so when I held my first child, squishy and little, I understood his desire to take that weight of the past, that threat of the future, and call it a new thing.

2.

It's dangerous to place your own dreams and desires on your children. They will carry enough from us already. We burden them with our phobias, our pain. We can't help it. They are easy targets. Loving. Trusting.

Like most parents, I dream a better world. I dream bike rides and farmer's markets. I dream collaboration and sustenance. Like most parents, I worry the future. I worry violence and rape. I worry technology. I both fear and desire separation. I imagine our home as oasis. The contours of which are never stable. The lesson I teach my children: never go close to the borders.

I've learned that for something to be born, there needs to be antecedents. How to rewild the world? How to stake claim? How to measure the distance between you and me? These are old questions, made more acute each generation. It's what we pass down. It's what we leave behind.

Sometimes I dream that things could be different, that the idea of enslavement never crossed the Atlantic, that belief in entitlement died on the cross, that the need to possess was a childish notion our parents freed us from.

3.

Any time I got a bloody nose as a young boy, I would let it bleed, let the blood run into my mouth, turn my teeth red, drip down my chin, savor the strange metallic taste, the oily consistency, the way it would dry on my skin. "Blood," my father always threatened. "Blood is what matters, blood is what makes you who you are." He'd hug me deep, whisper like a warning, "You are my blood," squeezing me till I hurt. "You my blood." In the mirror, alone I'd repeat, "My blood, my blood," over and over until the words lost meaning.

4.

Here's a story: I remember the day I read an article about the history of science and how it's not neutral, that it's been shaped by social values such as racism and patriarchy. I sat in a waiting room ignoring my young son, my pregnant but sick girlfriend next to me. We were made to wait, unable to schedule an appointment because we were on medi-cal, told that priority was given to insured patients. We were 23 and 24. We said ok. While we waited, I read this article about fertility. I remember wondering where does knowledge come from? At some point in my life I learned or came to believe that sperm actively hustled their little tails off to plunder the fallopian tubes chasing down wary passive eggs to penetrate, to impregnate. The article argued that that narrative depended on gendered assumptions about male, about female. My son meanwhile running wild in the waiting room. My girlfriend looking irritated trying to nap. The article declared that the egg, in fact, had its own hustle, its own agency, embodied its own will to find sperm, to become fertilized. Can egg choose sperm? By default, I wondered can egg reject sperm or sperm, egg. My son now crying on the floor. I let him. Loud and angry. We were seen almost immediately. I remember learning two things: screaming kids get you seen quicker and how wrong I was. I remember wondering what else I may not know. Or worse, not know what I think I already know. The word is mistaken.

Fathering is an art. Part tragedy, Part farce. If you do it well, you do it so they leave. You do it so you empty out; you do it knowing in the end, you are alone. An end and a beginning. Fathering gave me the ability to love and broke my heart. Verified deep in the body, the axiom: it is not about who or what loves you, it's the loving you do that matters.

At my doctor whom I visited because I developed, soon after my youngest daughter left, an inability to sleep deeply. I tossed. I turned. Incessantly. I felt hot. Overheated. I shared with him that perhaps I was under stress. Alone. Lonely. The doctor shared that his youngest had too just departed for college. I said, "How are you feeling?" The Doctor said, "Better than I thought." The Doctor said, "I think that our kids in fact wean us though we tell ourselves we are letting them go." The Doctor promises that I'm fine. Asks if I want sleeping pills. I don't but I say, "Yes." I like the thought of being weaned. The sacrilege of child parenting parent.

5.

I romanticize resistance. In my late 20s, I checked out from the library every book I could about indigenous uprisings, escapes, and especially victories. I read about the Iroquois, the Cheyenne, the Navajo, the Apache, the Nez Perce, the Modoc. In 1992, a newly arrived resident of the Bay Area, I attended the anti-Columbus Day protests scattered through North Beach, the historically Italian part of the city. I ran the sidewalks while pushing my 2-year-old son in one of those fold up strollers. He squealed in delight while I fell in love: enamored by resistance embodied through visibility. My first experience with the black bloc, masked rioters, aerosol terrorists, armed with a blatant hatred for the police. Genderless aggression.

My son, a few years later, informed me he needed to make a model mission. I speak with the teacher. I'm told, "It's a state mandate." I'm told, "There is no choice." My son says, "It's fine Dad." He says it in that way he pleads for me to step back, desperate for me not to make a scene. "Fine," I tell the Teacher. We make it. It's the best damn mission, complete with indigenous burial ground.

In 2015, the Pope canonized Junípero Serra, the person responsible for the missions along the coast of California. The guilty party. Beatified sickness. Perhaps I should call the land Mexico, or the mythical Aztlán of my Chicano nationalism or further back to the Ohlone who called this area Costanoan. The power of naming. My son texts me, "Didn't we go to some protest against this dude?" "We did," I text. "Do you remember? Do you?"

6.

Sometimes I feel like the same things happen over and over again just with different outcomes.

7.

When Bay Street Shopping Mall opens in Emeryville in 2001 on both a burial ground of indigenous people and an ancient Shellmound, I refuse to go. For years I never went. It housed the new movie theater; it builds in popularity. IKEA opens. Then, H&M, Urban Outfitters. My daughter says she understands and that she will just go with her mother. Of course, I begin taking them. I fear being left out. I fear not being relied on. I fear they won't love me.

Sometimes what can you do. Sometimes you lose. Sometimes all you can do is hold onto the names. Use them like they are natural, like they are capable of capturing the whole truth, telling the whole story: the victories and the losses, the story behind the stories.

8.

In April 2013 I wrote a poem about my mother:

Nipples

> My mother never wore a bra; instead, she regularly wore shirts that said: *flat is beautiful* or *boobies are for babies*, her little breasts hanging low, her nipples arrogant, hard, always poking through the material. It embarrassed me. When I was fifteen, I asked her as she was getting dressed, "Why, Mom, why don't you even own a bra?" She turned to me shirtless and asked, "Do you know the reason men have nipples?" "No," I shrugged. She said, "To remind them of what they could have been."

A year later I wrote a poem about my father:

Scars

> "Do you want to see a match burn twice," my father asked me one day. We were sitting on the couch. We were alone, a rare occasion. Knowing my father, I was certain it was a trap, but said ok anyway. I craved the attention. He took out his matchbook, something he always had on him, sliding it from the pack of Kools. He struck a match and it sizzled into a flame. He let it burn. A match burning is a beautiful thing. Like a fist unfurling. I watched, waiting. He looked at me and then back at the burning match. I heard him inhale and blow it out. Then without hesitating he touched the ember, orange and glowing, to my forearm. "Get it," he laughed, "It burned twice." It's a trick that can only work once. I often wonder how long he waited to play it on me. I marvel at his patience, his determination every time I touch the scar.

It only occurred to me after that I was rewriting, perhaps retelling, something about myself. Where I came from. From whom. My mother never used those words exactly but she said similar things over and over again. Does that make sense? Before I read at open mics, I obfuscate: these pieces are half autobiographical fiction and half fictional autobiography. How to explain?

9.

I obsess about origin stories. How there once was nothing. And then there is something. Perhaps there will be something after that. The way even the idea expressed in english forces verb tense changes. *Was* now *is* now *will be.* "A word after a word after a word is power," writes Margaret Atwood. To begin and to end is one and the same.

10.

I often say fathering made me a feminist but I should also add that I grew into manhood through fathering as well and so had to somehow balance the two things together. Surprisingly, it wasn't that hard because I actually think the two go hand in hand, that they are closely entwined with each other. At least they are for me.

But there were some key moments that highlighted how masculinity under patriarchy set me up to fail, to internalize misogyny as natural, to embody male privilege.

Here's an example: as a young father I loved roughhousing with my son tickling and tackling and rolling around despite what he said when we were doing it. A little later on I roughhoused with my daughter (and, of course, I made sure to roughhouse equally with both of them), but when she said stop through her laughter, I immediately did, knowing how crucial it was that I listened to her words, that I stopped. It hit me then: how when my son said no, I didn't immediately listen to him. It haunts me to this day, the lesson that his words didn't matter, that I could ignore his expressed desire to stop. It's a failure on my part. What did he learn about consent, about boundaries? What I taught him was exactly what my father had taught me. Be a man.

I realize I need role models of other men doing the difficult work of reclaiming masculinity, reconsidering their own relationship to manhood, sharing and exploring how they learned (sometimes painfully, sometimes humorously) what being a man means despite what society wants us to believe.

11.

Too often we fail to say what we mean. How to speak what resides in the creases of your palms or in the scar your father gave you? Share with me the word that captures all you see in the dark. Sadly, there is simply too much violence in the world for me to just touch you without asking or perhaps fear stays my hands. Either way some things the body speaks more clearly. Instead, we learn to voice desire, name boundaries, call out for support, cry justice. But the body understands intrinsically, knows we cannot speak our way to empathy; we embody it. I remember as a young man the first few nights I took my son home from the hospital. I remember the way he cried, not painful, not hungry, just sort of lonely. At first, I spoke to him. I called him his name. But he continued to cry. Then I picked him up. I held his naked body against mine. This did something for him because he soon fell asleep, but what has stayed with me, deep in my own body, is what holding that crying baby did for me.

12.

Sometimes I feel like I write the same thing over and over again just with different words.

13.

Driving through what we now call Montana, I am reminded of what names came before, what stories lie buried beneath the plains. I visit the memorials of men I abhor, of battles I wish were never fought. I learn stories to tell my children. For example, imagine the strength it took Crazy Horse to witness his daughter born and choose the name They Are Afraid of Her knowing as he did she probably never stood a chance. When I wonder how to survive, I think of my children and understand that I already have.

When You Insist I'm Mexican, You Bring Out the Guatemalan in Me

Gabriela Ramirez-Chavez

After Cisneros

When you insist I'm Mexican,
you bring out the Guatemalan in me.
The memories of the past.
Civil War cries.
The frijoles negros blood.

Hear, all Latinos are not the same.
Words fly from my tongue like
calidad, chilero, puchicas vos,
rape, disappearance, torture.

A green Quetzal, I sing silence.
Feel my El Petén rainstorms of fury,
the hatred of state-sanctioned violence
and US-intervention are in me.

When you insist I'm Mexican,
you bring out the Ix Chel
moon goddess in me.
La Siguanaba seductress.
The dark sands of San Jose.

See, sí, I am
la viuda, planchadora, tamalera.
El comal y la pila.
La pata rajada y Maya huipil.
The K'iche' fire tongue.
The indígena and ladina.
The victim and conqueror.

White Dog, Femur Shrinking

D.M. Chávez

Driving along the Mississippi
my father's words return,
Stand up tall. Back straight.
Shoulders broad.
Suck in your stomach.
Head high and proud.
"What's the matter, Dear?
Is your femur shrinking?"
my elder friend, Elle, teases
because I told her
in my smart ass days,
it had to be her spine
since she couldn't
have lost four inches
from her legs. Yet, I,
who've only ever stood up
taller than my height,
learned last week
I've lost a half inch
somewhere in my travels.

More than twenty years ago
in Azusa, California, a fellow editor,
Jefferson Davis told me the story
of the white dogs they chained
to posts in front yards
in parts of the South
—trained to hate blacks,
to go rabid-crazy if
a black man came in sight of,
setting foot on white property.

When Michelle Spears and I
went to J.D.'s Christmas party,
we were the only two people
of color in the living room.

She was "lemon-skinned,
like my illustrious grandfather,"
she told me, and wore
her hair in a big reddish afro,
so no one would accuse her
of trying to pass.
As for me, I'm told I have
Aztec, Apache, Navajo
and European bloods; and
no one's ever been able
to figure me out. So they've said,
one way and another
inviting me to their parties,
claiming me, while I've been
young and, I guess,
relatively smooth and
arguably pretty, in the way
some say even the plainest
young people are pretty
when they're practically babies.

As I age, I know Persian men
won't continue to pester,
"Are you sure you're not
Persian?" And Asian women
will stop insisting, "Remember
the Bering Strait; your
ancestors were also Asian."
While Europeans will
stop declaring, "You're
part French, obviously,"
and "Obviously,
you have German."

German? Really? When
they're obnoxious enough
I don't tell them about
the aristocracy of my forebears
who might as well have been
among those who tainted
so much of what they touched,
only how any of us could also be
Mestizaje – after all, some Aztecs
blended with Africans, as did

some New Mexican Spaniards
where my Apache and Navajo
forebears lived and aren't buried
under church altars. Who knows?

One white woman driving a group
to a prayer meeting tried so hard
to nail it down while she drove.
"Well, what kinds of foods
did they feed you in your
home of origin?" she probed,
looking up at me in her rear view
mirror. "Hamburgers," I replied.
It was partly true, and she had it
coming. The others grinned
surveying the scenery. With that
she let it drop in the middle
of the road. *Thud.*

If it wasn't obvious enough
to us and others that Michelle
and I were the only two
people of color on the couch,
in the kitchen, or by the bar
at the party, a white Shih Tzu
came and barked at Michelle.
It would not stop barking,
though it didn't carry on
snarling at anyone else.
Perhaps they were all familiar,
family and friends. But the way
it persisted, and how it refused
to cease, was something.

"Honey," said J.D.'s wife,
who never did offer more than
a hello to Michelle, "Put her out,
won't you?" But the white dog
got back inside. When the little shit-
zu climbed up onto my lap
to growl at my friend's big
auburn fro, I looked at Michelle
and asked, "Want to leave?"
Michelle nodded. I handed off

the little pest. Outside on the porch
we said our goodbyes to J.D.
wishing him "Merry Christmas."

We laughed it off
but didn't say much
on the freeway back.
Twenty years later, I drive
one of many bridges over this
wide hot chocolate river.
My father's voice returns,
Sit up tall, back straight,
as I move to adjust my seat.
My elder friend, Elle, turns to me.
She's simpering again, "What's
the matter, Dearie?
Femur still shrinking?"
I stretch out my legs
while driving, and feel
how strong they are.

Nepantlando ────────────────

Soy Hija de Coyote   Inés Hernández-Avila

I have always moved among worlds,
I have never known otherwise.
Nepantlera soy
    I walk around every day
        knowing I am a descendant of Chief Joseph's band
         of the Nimipu/Nez Perce
           knowing I am one of a few thousand alive from this line
          does anyone care?
               Do my grandchildren care?
                 Do they know what it means?
                   Can they speak to it?
                   Joseph
                   Hinmaton Yalatkit
                   comes to me
                   in spirit
                   I trust his presence
                   In my life
                   Thunder Rolling
                   Over the Mountains

                   The smell of Indian-cured
                   buckskin takes me home
                   to my Grampa Tom
                   playing his drum
                   singing

not from the reservation
thankful for the deep ties
my mom gave me
only some Nimiputimki
words
where is my Nimipu voice?
my Nimipu heart is strong
Coyote strong
            Coyote is the Original Nepantler@
Knowing in my body
the history of our people

from the beginning of time
moved within my core
by the songs of the
Seven Drums
and yet

I am lonely

As a Nimipu
As a Nepantlera
As a mexicana

not my sons
not my grandchildren
not my husband
relate to Mexicanness the way I do
me encanta hablar en español
me encanta cantar en español
the other colonizer's language
yes

I am moved by Mexico
I radiate with Mexico
Am I tied to that earth in some special way?
I am drawn to Mexico so.
the songs, the rhythms, the sounds, the food, the people
las historias de revolución
I could go anywhere in the world
but I am drawn to Mexico so much.
Is it the Tejana in me?

Ay, Mamá Inés / Ay, Mamá Inés / Todos los negros / Tomamos café.

Home
where is home
I too am a turtle
where have I felt at home
Galveston
Cuba
Puerto Rico
Yucatán
Venezuela
the waters
Gulf of Mexico
Yemaya
Reina del Mar

Patrona de los Pescadores
azul y blanco
tus colores
Diosa de nosotras
las que sabemos navegar las aguas
las que hemos sobrevivido
las tempestades más violentas
las que tenemos tu fuerza
dentro de nuestro ser

O mi Yemaya / quítame lo malo / quítame lo malo / déjalo en el mar

Suspiro Respiro
Pienso en las montañas, los ríos
Se me viene a mi ser
Mi otra parte

Inside the sweat lodge
within ceremony
singing singing singing
dripping with sweat
cleansing
drinking the tea
praying praying
coyote songs bear songs
earth songs
little eagle songs
dancing dancing
ceremonially
standing up
inside the lodge
dancing praying
breathing fire
praying
inside the arbor
dancing
seeing the ancestor spirits
praying
in the heavens
praying

dancing
bailes tejanos
música cubana
African music
Salsa

Cajun
Accordion
Vallenato
dancing
sacred healings
I was born dancing
I will cross over
dancing

How do I renew myself within Nepantla?
What do I do to stay whole?
Garden feel the earth,
Garden dig my hands deep in the earth
care for my plants
love them talk to them
ask them to teach me
I paint
find my self
me libero
me invento a mí misma
Moyocoyatzin
Me acerco al Ser Supremo
A las diosas
a ese misterio que tiene
tant@s nombres
I love the idea of
the Mystery.

I am alone in Nepantla,
very alone
Who understands me
does it matter?
La vereda de la vida
ultimadamente
es
solitaria.

"y sin que nadie lo sepa / viday / me voy llorando"
dice Atahualpa
pero también
voy cantando

Moving, moving, moving, Coyote moving,
daughter of Coyote moving,
Huehuecoyotl be with me,
Enséñame como vivir, vibrar,

to pulsate con armonía
al son de la danza de la vida,
let me dance, walk, breathe
effortlessly
each dance is mine,
I have the palabra,
so that I am impeccable
here in Nepantla,

Si me tropiezo, tengo que levantarme, como lo hice una vez bailando en Chalma—me caí cuando estaba llevando mi danza, todo el mundo me estaba siguiendo, me dió harta pena. I got up, kept dancing, this was my palabra, I did not give up, I did not leave my obligation, mi compromiso, I kept going. I hurt tremendously afterwards—un jefe de la danza me dió una de esas sobadas that turned my world on its head, but I finished my dance, I have done this so many times in Nepantla, been knocked down, been dismissed, been overlooked, when I'm right here in Nepantla, maybe *because* I'm in Nepantla I have been set aside, I appear not certain, without a side, without a position, but my position is Nepantla, right here, moving, shifting, contemplando, considerando, as I move, as I feel, feeling, feeling, feeling, not being emotional, but having sensibilidad y conciencia—contempl*ando*. I need to feel what is right for me. No soy partidaria. No soporto a la política de patrones ni patronas. No sigo lineas que me parecen muchas veces muy rígidas. I get up, I always get up, it's in my blood to get up, as a Nimipu woman, as my parent's daughter, as Coyote's daughter, as a Nepantlera.

Within this world, there has been treachery from those who I could consider my own, those who claim a consciousness I also want to have.

Colleagues
Elders
Spiritual people
Compañer@s en la lucha
Raza
Indígena
y Mexicana
Ni
modo.

Conciencia. Con razón, Corazón. How did I know way back what the truth was? How did I know that it is the path of the heart, like the Yoeme maso who leaves a flower everywhere he steps, everywhere she steps. Moving gracefully, creating a flower world, bringing it in, letting us feel it, so that we can be renewed. Renew, renew, renew, paint, paint, create, write, write about my self, write about my life, what will I write, how will I write? I am secretive, a recluse, shy, really, although to many I would not seem thus. La vida me ha enseñado protegerme. I know enough to know that things are not always what they seem. Se me vuelan cuando alguien piensa que me puede engañar, when someone tries to play me. Does the rage in me surface too easily? Does it border on madness? Am I becoming less patient the older I get? Am I sometimes too abrasive when I speak? Do I give myself permission to speak up? I ask for the light of compassion to flow over me and through me. Is there a reason for me to feel fear?

Fear, fear, fear, not being good enough,
not being valid,
being in-valid.
Invalid.
I want to be whole
on my terms, not on anyone else's

been there done that the other way
can't live someone else's life
someone else who doesn't exist
I need to live my own painful joyful life
como Nepantlera Tejana Nimipu Coyote
not my mother's not my father's not my sons'.
I want them to understand me
Is that possible?
Did I truly understand my father?
My mother?
I think I did.
I think I knew them, know them.
Did I?
is that ever really possible?

I want to be the person my spirit wants me to be,
one with my spirit,
my mind, my heart, my will, my body.
My body, cómo te hecho sufrir
Mi cuerpo, no siempre te defendí
no siempre te he cuidado
has aguantado golpes
sufrimiento
violación
dolor
por
falta
de conciencia
con lágrimas
amargas
y llenas de amor
te pido perdón

Why did I internalize so much poison?
Why did I let it come into me?
Heal myself
heal myself
heal.

Healing is spiritual work.
Estando en el centro
llamando a los buenos espíritus
de las cuatro direcciones
la tierra el cielo
el centro
pido
Ancestor
friend
spirit guide
beloved animal relation
Come to me
hear me
listen
let me listen
with ears of the heart that find you
let me see with eyes of the heart that go so far beyond
let me look into myself
with the hands of the sacred
with eyes of the sacred
with heart of the sacred

Help me have love
radiate from all my being
in blues purples fuschias greens
marigolds turquoise
Love love love
of myself
others

life
the universe
My body is music
My cells are singing
I dance
My spirit dances
My spirit dances love
My spirit dances
My spirit heals.

To Mexico City's Raging Aztec

Nidia Melissa Bautista

Your skin, as you so correctly pointed out, is indeed lighter than mine. A lighter, more yellow, tone of brown. These shades of brown aren't the only borders that separate us. The differences between how we speak and what we sound like are as thick as the rusted metal plates that catch the gleam of golden sunsets in Tijuana.

You Chilango, speak Nahuatl. I Pocha, speak Spanglish. Although on days when I need to put on a more authentic performance of my Mexicanness, I pull out my seven years of (un)learning Spanish to pass just as you do. Cuauhtémoc is your martyr, you consider Tenochtitlán usurped, Cortés a bastard, Trump a bigot, and are frustrated and angry and consider everything culturally constructed around you in the last 500 years a terrible joke.

And I agree with you, on the frustration, disdain, and pain of seeing, and being one of a few who have survived the destruction of what you consider the true expression of your authentic self. But you raging at me in Nahuatl on the metro is not fucking okay.

It went down like this: Riding the metro on a January evening, a friend and I discussed the excitement and unease brought on by the start of a new year in the city. Two transplants in Mexico City by way of Los Angeles and San Diego, Mexico City to us is the current cultural and political mecca of our creativity and lives. For my friend a photographer and I a writer, it was a long time coming.

We were riding northbound on a packed Line 2 train, squeezed between students and office employees, discussing our plans for the year. And as naturally as Spanglish rolls off my tongue in the middle of Broadway in Downtown LA, and as easy it is to integrate the colloquial slang of my campesino grandfather in my conversations with elder Chilangxs in a coffee shop in Colonia Portales, I spoke English with my friend on the metro. Laughing and discussing our plans, our conversation was suddenly interrupted by the grunts and mumbling of a man sitting in the row directly in front of us. Unphased we continued with our conversation until it was again abruptly interrupted with the man's husky voice exclaiming, "Fuck!" followed by his incoherent mumbling.

Suddenly aware of his anger at us, we became tense as we pretended to ignore him. Our resilience to continue on with our conversation, one that fluidly switched to Spanish and Spanglish, infuriated him further. Suddenly made brave, and impatient to this man's anger at us, I turned and stared squarely at him. Locking eyes, he pulled up his sleeve to show me the pale brown color of his wrist and inner arm and said to me in Spanish, "Can't you see? I'm lighter than you and I speak Spanish. I speak Nahuatl too! Do you speak Nahuatl?"

Left dumbfounded, my friend jumped to respond and scolded the man for eavesdropping and even interrupting our conversation. At this point, having broken that immaculate and entrancing silence that characterizes metros all over the world, we had the attention of the entire car. Eager to avoid this confrontation, I turned back to my friend and we resumed our conversation, except now my anxious voice increasingly integrated Spanish. Unrelenting, the man continued to rant at us, accusing us of pretending English fluency, scolding us to be ashamed, us two dark brown womxn, at having embraced English as it's the language of Donald Trump.

There, a full-out quadrilingual argument ensued on the metro of Mexico City. In our exchange, I explained that Trump was a racist, sexist pig and not at all representative of an entire language and country (perhaps half-heartedly because maybe he DOES and maybe that's exactly why the US is the most terribly racist country in the world). I explained my family's history of migration. I explained that like myself, thousands of Mexicans in the US don't speak Nahuatl and still live the spiritual and material violence promoted by Trump. I explained, with a nervous and infuriated voice, that that doesn't make me any less, or anymore, Mexican.

Unsatisfied, the man went from scolding us like an elder, to scolding us like pochas.

Unauthentic, arrogant, shameless, embarrassment. All these things I'm sure he threw at us in Nahuatl. Our exchange lasted about three metro stops, when he decided to end the conversation and stand up to get off at his stop. And amidst awkward giggles and sighs, we let him know it was our stop too, and followed right behind him.

Getting off the train and away from the suffocating silence and probing stares of fellow passengers, we walked off and toward the exit, tense and contemplative. Such an intimate and intense confrontation and discussion, one I have dedicated essays and much meditation on, made quickly public.

Not belonging to either nationalism, but to the local experience of my life in Boyle Heights and joy and heartbreak in Mexico City. Choosing to embrace my transfronteriza existence came after five years of traveling between Mexico City and Los Angeles. Facing constant questioning of my accent, the confusion of having "perfect English" despite such brown skin, the ruthlessly violent nationalism of the US's immigration policy toward Mexicans and Mexico's increasing deportation and violence against Central Americans, the classism embedded in the social fabric of Mexico City and the self-hate of my diaspora anxious to succeed and be visible in the institutions del otro lado. My life navigating nationalism led to my commitment only to the transbarrio. To the value and connection of our experiences as people pumping with life and love and not limited to our possession of a passport, a passing accent or knowledge of either English or Spanish, or of an adequate performance to please a perpetually displeased authenticity police.

The anxiety of facing and being spiritually defeated by the Aztec in Mexico City's metro opens these wounds and reminds me of the pain that like a border still unites us. His anger fueled by a racism and nationalism all his own, all still present and ephemeral in the streets of this city and in the probing stares of our elders in our hoods of Los Angeles and New York City. Gentrification, displacement, colonialism, patriarchy, violence, hate, nationalisms, borders, mis-understanding.

Years of colonialism and imperialism sustain the meta-border that still separates and divides us.

For our diasporas, when it comes to melanin and identity, language and perfor-mativity, nothing is ever just one shade of belonging, neither Pocha nor Aztec. Like the diversity of the brown gleaming faces of school children in playgrounds in Boyle Heights, our essence is of endless promise, endless forms to be. We wear jade around our wrists, huaraches or sometimes jelly sandals on our feet, hand-woven rebosos and leather jackets frame our shoulders, nostalgia pumps in our hearts, and Zapotec hip-hop, Nahuatl prose, Spanish scoldings, Spanglish epiphanies enlighten our mornings and nights in our hoods and campos.

All this left unspoken in a metro car filled with hate and anxiety
Coming back to healing and meditation
Reaffirming that what unites us can be more powerful
and conducive to collective healing than what divides
Still searching for those spoken words to help this healing
Still I build the strength and peace to continue this journey in my current
Nepantla capital

Articulating "homeland"
A sensuous and political journey

Nadine Saliba

I said: Where are you taking me?
He said: Toward the beginning, where you were born.

Mahmoud Darwish

The union that begat me was a marriage made across borders. My Syrian mother, Georgette, crossed national borders into Lebanon to wed my father Nahil, a history teacher whom she never tires of teasingly reminding that Lebanon used to be part of Greater Syria before the colonial powers occupied and divided the region after World War One. Upon getting married, my parents lived in the seaport city of Tripoli, located on the eastern shore of the Mediterranean Sea in North Lebanon.

Tripoli is endearingly referred to as *al-Faihaa*—the Fragrant One. The adjective comes from the verb *faha,* which means to diffuse a strong and beautiful smell. The city got its nickname from the orange orchards surrounding it. During the blooming season, the air carries the fragrance of orange blossoms across the city, filling its neighborhoods and suburbs with a splendid smell. I was too young when we lived in Tripoli to remember this, but smell is said to be the most advanced sense that babies have. Whenever I think about the city of my birth, I ask my parents to tell me again about that orange blossom smell drifting to our balcony with the wind wandering inland from the sea.

Tripoli is an ancient city dating back to the 14th Century BCE. It was fought over, conquered, and swallowed by the expanding borders of many empires in ancient and modern times. The city was a major Phoenician port before it fell under Assyrian, Persian, Greek, Roman, Byzantine, Arab, Muslim, Crusader, Ottoman, and French rule. These civilizations left behind echoes of their passing, creating a world whose identity has never been closed off or barricaded. Beneath the history of conflicts and imperial conquests persists a less visible historical record populated by cross-fertilization, cultural exchange, and the traffic of ideas across geographic and temporal borderlines.

I was born to a city with a rich but burdensome history. After World War One, France and Britain divided the Arab world creating the borders that exist today. Tripoli was one of the victims of these new borders imposed by foreign powers.

Once an economic and commercial center with the pride of history and the splendor and record of a thriving city, the new map-makers wrenched it from its natural environment, cutting it off from the Syrian interior with which it had centuries-old economic, trade, cultural, and social ties. They annexed it to modern-day Lebanon, where it has been systematically marginalized by a highly centralized state. Sociologists, political analysts, and the records of the United Nations tell us that Tripoli today is the poorest city on the Mediterranean Sea with over half of its population living below the poverty line.

This is the city I was born to but separated from by war.

I was a child when my father, fearing sectarian strife after the outbreak of the Lebanese civil war, decided to leave Tripoli and move back to his village. So I grew up in a small village in the el-Koura district. The area squats on a series of foothills and plains sprinkled with what may be the largest uninterrupted olive groves in the world, yielding thick-textured, dark green olive oil whose fame traveled beyond its borders.

The smell from my childhood of freshly-picked olives rises from the recesses of my memory. Defying distance, it transports me to an old one-room stone structure not far from our house, where my sister and I used to go watch a dying art as olives were pressed not by a machine but by a gargantuan stone mill pulled in circles by a beast of burden. The odor is so pervasive it swaggers in my nostrils, it owns me.

I did not know then that the olive tree bore my visceral and spiritual connection to Palestine even before the Palestinian struggle entered my political consciousness. In token of an unbroken connection, I was ritualistically anointed during my baptism with *Myron* made from myrrh, aromatic spices, and remnants of Palestinian olive oil pressed from fields harvested from the time Jesus walked through them.

So I grew up in the countryside, separated from Tripoli by a mere 30-minute drive and a stubborn sectarian divide. While many areas in Lebanon were physically cut off from each other during the war, the divide between a majority-Muslim Tripoli and a majority-Christian el-Koura was not a physical border, it was a state of mind.

All wars are tragic but there is no war more tragic or ruinous than a civil war and no conflict more ravaging than a sectarian conflict as it rips at a country's social fabric like the de-skinning of a live animal. I couldn't wait to grow up and vomit all of it. Perhaps that was my first border crossing, clawing my way out of the mental, physical, and spiritual walls erected with ideas and habits normalized by that war. Intricately, I unknit my values one thread at a time and wrote myself anew.

It did not take me long after arriving in San Antonio to realize that I left one borderland for another. After all, the city bears in the Alamo the marker of a border imposed by conquering powers. Place is emotion and every geography in my atlas has been a source of pain. How closely does today's bleeding border resemble yesterday's. The US-Mexico border is an open wound, said Gloria Anzaldúa, "where the third world grates against the first and bleeds. And before a scab forms, it hemorrhages again the life blood of two worlds, merging to form a third country, a border culture."

Just like the olive trees in my village took me to Palestine once, Palestine brought me back to San Antonio, whispering its pre-colonial name in my ear, Yanaguana. And so I realized that my story did not begin in 1975 with the Lebanese war, or in 1967 with my mother's displacement from her ancestral home in the Syrian Golan Heights, not even in 1948 with the Palestinian Nakba. My story began in 1492 because Palestine is a metaphor for the post-1492 settler colonial world where "the bulldozers of history," to borrow Darwish's term, have been engaged in a project of existential and cultural erasure against indigenous people. Because we read the Palestinian story within the global narrative of colonial conquest, resistance and the struggle for justice, my story begins in 1492.

Self-definition is a political act. So I weave an intimate relationship with my current geography and create kinship with the place through ties of solidarity with its people spun from historical connections and shared political values and struggles. I claim San Antonio as homeland too because it is the Palestine of my "new world." Chance brought me to this city but she was waiting for me. Revealing herself, she said, I'm not a stranger to you. You know me, you will recognize me, I bear traces of your history on my body.

But that place "where you were born" doesn't leave you either. It tugs at your soul like a child holding on to her mother's dress. And perhaps like most immigrants, we try to recreate home any way we can. In our family, we've attempted to grow a piece of it in our garden where, if you come visit us, you will find grape vines, fig, olive, pomegranate, apricot, and almond trees as well as mint, parsley, thyme, and oregano. Odors are unruly; they don't respect boundaries and are always on the move. They inundate you without warning or permission. If you come in the spring, you will be invaded by the scents of jasmine, damascene roses, orange and lemon blossoms.

Aromas penetrate our consciousness, providing us with a fluid experience of space and time. Our bodies carry the scent of places we've been to and people we've embraced. When we leave, odors hang on to our bodies, translating the shape of the place and the spirit of the people. They are nature's way of defying a harsh reality of distance and separation.

The scent of Arabian jasmine on the window sill in our backyard puts me on the marble steps in the spacious garden of my father's cousin on hot summer nights, with relatives and neighbors visiting. My mother is there too, smoking. There must've been no other children because I'm not playing and running around.

Instead, I am wearing a bright-colored dress that mama made from floral fabric and sitting with one pretentious leg over the other as my clog barely hangs off my foot.

Almond blossoms, on the other hand, take me to the street outside our house, too narrow for pedestrians to be safe when a car whizzes by. It's a chilly early morning on a spring day. I am waiting for my daily ride to school but, today, I can smell the fragrance of almond blossoms in the garden of our neighbor, the priest. It doesn't last long at all, maybe a week or two. I've never smelled something so beautiful since.

Comedy Curanderismo

Monica Palacios

Walking on stage was no problem. I could handle that. It was facing the audience, strangers who I knew were homophobic, racist, and sexist based on how much they laughed at the comic ahead of me who trashed queers, women, and Latinos. I didn't want to be at these clubs that promoted hate as an art form, but I needed stage time to work out my new profession as a comic in the summer of 1982 in San Francisco.

Here I was in the gayest city in the world, but these mainstream clubs were not welcoming to LGBTQ people. Yes, I was an out lesbian but I never did queer material at straight clubs because I never felt safe. Homophobia was rampant and AIDS exacerbated this fear and hate of queer folks. At the clubs you could count on straight male comics doing AIDS jokes—two words that should never go together.

I happened to pick up the gay newspaper Bay Area Reporter where I found an ad promoting "Gay Comedy Open Mic Night" at The Valencia Rose Cabaret 766, Valencia Street in The Mission. I immediately thought: These are my peeps. This is my place. I must go here and perform. But then I thought: If I perform here, I'm going to be known as a lesbian comedian and that could ruin my career. As if I had a career! I had only performed stand-up comedy a few times. But being in the closet was what one did to survive in the '80s, especially in the entertainment industry. I thought about going and not going to the Valencia Rose for one long week and then concluded: fuck it—I'm a badass Chicana dyke!

I walked into the Valencia Rose with nervous confidence and was greeted by the MCs Tom Ammiano and Carol Roberts. Both were very nice and Tom gave me the rules: "No homophobic, racist, sexist, fat, or disabled jokes." Sounded good to me.

I did the same set I had been doing at the straight clubs but this time I was a full blown jota. I was ridiculous, bold, sexy, kooky, and proudly out! It felt incredibly empowering to be my whole self. The audience was loving my material—they were loving me! These LGBTQ people were in hysterics and when I finished, they burst out in thunderous applause. I had just experienced my first spiritual group hug.

After my set, all the comics came up to me with praise. I'm not going to lie, being the highlight of the night was a fierce turn on. At this sacred queer space

I was able to be my self 100%. I didn't have to hide my dyke within as I did a week earlier when I performed at the Punchline, where I felt super unsafe and in a nervous state of mind I said into the microphone, "My boyfriend and I...," I felt sick for days. The Valencia Rose was my new casa de queers.

The Rose allowed me to strengthen my comedy muscle. I was building a following. I had fans! My performances were attracting a lot of attention because I was funny, bold, and rare: Chicana lesbian comic from Califas. San Jose born and raised. I was a home girl. I was a homo home girl.

I was steadily getting hired by LGBTQ activists and organizations and straight political Latino organizations would hire me for their annual awards dinners. I would take these Latino gigs because I needed the money and I wanted to perform for my raza but I never did any queer material. I never felt safe at these particular events. Usually I would perform with one or two male Latino comics who would do homophobic jokes that the audience found hilarious. This totally sucked and was a punch in the gut minutes before I went on stage. I wanted to be fully embraced by mi raza, instead I was treated like a second-class citizen.

Latinos weren't the only homophobes. Once, a few of us queer comics performed at a Gay Comedy Night at UC Berkeley. The white jocks in the audience became so verbally hostile towards us, the police were called in to escort us to our cars.

My Chicana lesbian feminist comedy career was constantly challenged in the '80s, the Decade of The Hispanic—which by the way lasted a couple of months. I was regularly told by heteros, "You're funny but get rid of the gay stuff. It's not going to get you anywhere." As I was receiving this thoughtless advice, I would experience racism from white LGBTQ groups or journalists who didn't understand why I didn't place more importance on my queer self. "I'm connected to my Chicana and lesbian identities at the same time. I'm never one without the other," I would inform them.

I was constantly "informing them" back in the day. Those were the dumb people. The cool people were supportive and found my work healing. It felt good performing my comedy curanderismo.

Black Card

Jennine DOC Wright

I've never had black girl magic
Never had brown girl brujeria
No, this is voodoo
Systematic sorcery, I cast system spells
Spit them out like the grito stuck in my throat…haaaaahhaahhaa ha ha
Sounds funny right?
Didn't think she could do that, thought she was black, there is no middle passage
    for mixed girls
And without a passage she ain't no essay, pretty sure I read her wrong
Never had a rite of passage, 15 passed right on by
A quinceañera is just a fiesta, a fee esta, a fee, a price, esta, to be
I have not yet appropriated myself, made me my own
When my mother died, I clenched at a culture never given
we weren't taught Spanish
It was only spoken around Christmas so we wouldn't know what we were getting
but it was a deliberate choice to not give something that would be taken away
Taken down the hall for special ed
Taken to the principal's office to stay after school
I never had to think too hard about how to copy sentences in only one language
We weren't given names with accents to be punished for having accents/
An accent is a mark indicating stress
And I have tried to pull my hair out but it is strong
The black girl in me is too proud to call it good
But it grows with just enough curl to be black sheep
This is the shit I'm not black enough or brown enough to talk about in public
How my Cesar Chavez heart beats in the MLK tomb in my chest
How I love chicken enchiladas and Tajín on my watermelon
How I'm not black enough for rhythm in my feet but my hips (have been coated salsa)
ooh she's spicy, she's exotic,
pick her African violet marigold skin pick her
This is how you flower tortillas and corn rows
stitching hood and barrio together, I am altered
hemming and hawing i guess because I'm tabled in cultural discussions so i am altered
skeletons in my closet, sugar coated calaveras
So i press King James against Virgin Mary palms
With confusion in not knowing when to jump up, hallelujah

and when to kneel
I pray, that when I am down I am heard the most
That my tongue is not so foreign that I'm met by a gatekeeper
Apparently I don't need a green card but I haven't earned a black one yet either
When my daughter was young she was excited to share Spanish, she recited
Uno, dos, tres, taco, (hahaha) I laughed at taco
How can I million man march when I can't get past four
some of you, right now have mental tally sheets
Just so you can tell which side I identify with more
There are people that say I only live half a struggle
they should recognize that there is more than just one

New Mexica Meditation

César L. De León

Somos		agua
Somos		tierra
Somos		fuego
Somos		aire
Somos		Alma
We are	salt	from the sea
We are	silt	from the river
We are	breath	from the four winds
We are	arrows	from the sun
We are	rabbits	of the moon
Somos	lengua	de serpiente
Somos	pluma	de quetzal
Somos	talón	de águila
Somos	hocico	de jaguar
Somos	canto	de cenzontle
We are	stalks	of corn
We are	thorns	of maguey
We are	rattle	of chile cascabel
We are	cactus	blossom
We are	sacred	smoke
Somos	la espiral	de la chicharra en el crepúsculo
Somos	el cosmos	reflejado en lajas de obsidian
Somos	raíces	profundas
Somos	raíces	entrelazadas
Somos	raíces	antiguas
Somos	raíces	nuevas
Somos	semillas	
We are	seeds	
Somos		semillas
We are	endless	roads
Somos	huellas	con memoria
We are	maps	sin fronteras

Somos puentes de luz.

secret

Nia Witherspoon

what if i'm not broken?

what if i'm just free?

not broken. just free.

not broken. free.

maybe a little broken.
but free.

breaking is freedom.

to break is to be free.

broken but free.

broken and free.

V

Allegory of the Rattlesnake

Joe Jiménez

1

Under sun, in debris: a cascabel hums its whole nautilus
of fangdom and scales—a harmony.

But it came for us, we said. We heard, and we'd heard:
      They can come for you. They will lash out. Animus:
      pain. And when it came—

As demon. As menace, as monolith, They as Goliath.

Everything we heard about rattlesnakes: the cascabel
made of God but less godly
      than us—

2

Understand this: Anyone can suffer.

3

In my most Mexican self, I understand the sun built a fire, for He once was a God
who said: the body cannot be dispensed
      unless I allow it. So I kneel,
so I show the sun my throat and hope He can fathom me whole.
      I'd suckle obsidian for a chance. At wholeness.
      But ardor. But fear. Ayotzinapa. But prayer. Ferguson like Juárez.

4

Until I learn to unlove arrangements that make me.
Until I hold a man in my mouth like a mouse or a cricket, a white moth, a whole hare.

5

It is no surprise. We refute wholeness.
Of those we believe will do us harm:

He deserved it, we said.
Look at the shit he'd done.
What was she wearing?
Had it coming, so many of us agreed.

6
Because fear is not an accident.

7
The ego of hissing. The bravado that is blabbering. The cascabel's teat-pink suit, its fang wilt and coil. Fiasco of scales and long rope.

Under debris, in sun: my body and his, yours and hers—
on asphalt, on hillsides, in trash heaps, in rivers, in fires in a great desert—

As demon. As menace, as monolith, They as Goliath.

Anywhere in the world—anyone can suffer.

SELF-PORTRAIT ACCORDING TO ──────
GEORGE W. BUSH

Roy G. Guzmán

In May 2006, Bush addressed a televised speech to the American public and Congress, pressing for stricter immigration laws. Language from that speech appears here.

[PINTURA/BLOOD]

Scent of fried flesh rolling over cracked white paint
as a young waitress, una
mejicana my age,
wipes the ketchup bottles with a coarse rag that resembles a bib.
I don't ask for her name

but I know she keeps an infant in one corner of the restaurant
where the patrons can't see it—day laborers, construction

workers—the prophet can be found anywhere, you see:
en la grieta, en el grito, in the knife

of the butcher in the kitchen, in the depluming
of the white lilies.

[ACEITES/WATERBOARDING]

For decades,
the Angel of Death says,
*the United States has not been in complete
control of its borders…*border as in
marca de zapatos de Payless for which I got a bloody
nose at school,

inner-city cymbals, halfway house doors,
la marca de la bestia in my queer vestiary, the brothel-home

where Mickey fucked us all, the immigrant's *Funeral*
March,
la mancha de mi país, el maricón who can't stop sweeping
roads with his tongue.

[REPRODUCCIONES/MELTING POT]

We will construct high-tech fences
in urban corridors, he says, como Dolphin Mall, como

Westland Mall en Hialeah, como Valsan—donde los que vienen
son mummified—to *build new patrol roads,*
                                        undetectable barbed
wire wound like colmillos on a clothesline
tied from one immigrant's feet

                    to another's, factories
where shame can be manufactured into appliances we can't afford,
where flesh billows the soul of a dream.

[MODELO/SURVEILLANCE SYSTEM]

            The baby's father has left the produce of his exile.

And she winks at me every time my parents stare at the dusty pictures
of players de fútbol on the wall, los machos
lionized. The owner
                is Chinese-Venezuelan-American
and has memorized our order—so that the hole in the wall
                    momentarily becomes our home in the wall.

The waitress excuses herself, as we conspire
by not acknowledging where the child's cries

                    come from. *Illegal immigrants live*
                    in the shadows of our society, La Muerte says,

but what can the voice learn from its echo
once the pronouncement has left the mouth?

[ACEITES/DDT POWDER]

The Texan uses verbs like *sneak* and insults like *criminals*
stayed	*broken*
verify	*beyond the reach*
enforce	*and protection of*
shut	*the American law*
secure	*debate*
apprehend	*human smugglers*
detain	*drug dealers*
catch	*risk*
confront	*terrorists*

> discourage   illegal immigrant
> assimilate   burden
> deport   "our friend"   —and yet

the deported will always forget to pack the second ghost
she never meant to give birth to, in a country
that now hates her—a ghost with which we must learn to cohabit,

> inhabit, let it possess our bones
> because that is what shame does
> with fence-material.

> For us, departure

will always signify the return to the unknown
language of *our neighbor* when he's gone.

[LUZ/BORDER PATROL]

On TV
        the mothers who look like mine, perhaps a little
lighter around the neck, wearing aviators, their faces
        sunburnt as they swear their allegiance to the cause:
help raid
        undocumented visionaries. The cameraman tries
to keep up with the one who moves like a tornado,
        as confident as anyone who's never faced
deportation.
        I turn to my parents, their silence bending in a cell.
Let's forget
        this woman's nationality for a minute. Let's say,
as an old roommate used to maintain, that all Latinos
        are to be loved because *y'all are so warm*—
perhaps because he's never
        known how some of us will bundle our fears
like do-rags over our heads, to cross a river that pummels
        like monochrome armies over our sovereignty.
The one time I've run
        with my demons packed in the trunk of a car
was when I volunteered
        at a nursing home, and my parents found out
I'd fallen for a boy's lips. High school existentialism.
        The boy had to sneak out when his parents
weren't home
        so he could call me from a payphone; from my end,
I had to keep my parents' English knowledge at a minimum.

Years later, that woman has moved in between
the channels. A ghost
　　　that mistakenly thinks the shamed body is the only
home she can know.
　　　She walks beside you like a tributary of penance.
As when I learned that you can love without the pretense
　　　of death, from anonymous men who would bite
hard into my nipples
　　　before they could spit out pubic hair. A wise friend
once said that a hen will almost always lose a chick
　　　on her way to the nail salon. The chick
will never kill
　　　his own brother, toss his body in a river, wait
until he hears
　　　about the crime from a stranger's facsimiled mouth.
Water levels rise like severed hands over the world's borders.
　　　Make no mistake that you will, in the humdrum,
forget what has haunted you.
　　　Then, one day, a sparrow will crack open the valves.
Bodies will swim under the furniture, on your neighbors'
　　　porch. The greenest ferns. And you will be there
alone to receive them—
　　　　　　　　not a part of your history spared.

[COLORES/DRONES]

BBQ Spare Ribs (5) costillas barbeque (5)..7.25
Estás caught otra vez entre qué comer today and the rest of the week because
you've started seeing a gastroenterologist and he's said we've got to be careful
about your colon because it's inflamed. Te recuerdas

Wonton Soup sopa de mariposas...2.00/3.00
of all the MSG you consumed in college, from that place with the bubble tea que
creo qu'is closed by now? They took away the Pizza Hut, left un McDonald's.
Some wounds nunca se abandonan tan easy. El frío

Hot & Sour Soup sopa picante y agria..4.00
of those Hyde Park streets nunca went away, as an extension of the art project
you turned out embodying, pero which you can't comprehend because you're
always living outside of it. Like a breeze en una bandera

Special Fried Rice especial de la casa 5.50/7.75/16.25
que se dobla y se dobla or a house que reza todas las noches for you not to come
back. Because la lengua del immigrant can wrap any leftovers, palos de guayaba,
pistas de aviones, el cura que nunca pudo bless you.

Chop Suey Chicken con pollo 6.00/7.75
And when you got a tu dorm, tu roommate te dice que his Russian is as rich
as Chekhov's, but he's not interested in the stories of possession you carry en tu
pecho de pelos que se enredan into huts para los que se escapan.

Chicken Lo Mein tallarines con pollo..6.00/8.50
You drive past los Home Depots, los restaurantes hondureños, y te entra una
tristeza to know that what connects you to your community is suspicion, regret,
el why didn't I go to school, el why you've been so lucky

Chicken w. Broccoli pollo con brócoli 6.00/8.00
que your parents never forced you to get a job, you could concentrate on your
materias, where would we be if we'd been given the same opportunities you've
had, although yo vivo in a house where I'm waiting

Shrimp w. Lobster Sauce camarones con salsa de langosta 6.50/9.50
for the master to return. I'm a wounded canino, can't you tell? Barking at myself
for not barking at the forms of trees. Tantos knots en la garganta como en los
zapatos one can't stop to loosen because one has to return

Sweet & Sour Chicken pollo agridulce...6.00/9.00
to work o te va a despedir el patrón. Tu madre begs you to stop spending your
money en chucherías, en going out con la otra gente de dinero, that's not why
you left Miami, that's not why she's detonating bombs on her back.

Soda refrescos... 1.00
But what she doesn't know is that loneliness is a symptom one becomes so adept
at concretizing in a foreign land, en el país de las manos rajadas,
where you eat a meal cooked by someone who has a similar story de huesos.

[SOMBRAS/DETENTION FACILITY]

A Chinese restaurant owner in Novi, Michigan,
houses five undocumented workers from Mexico
in the basement of his residence. Wages under
a clean bathtub. Every meal stirred by silence.
Their ages: 16, 18, 18, 23, and 23 to demonstrate
that death likes to show off in odds and pairs.
The fire begins as an unheard prayer over an old
mattress, and spreads like wild deer once it is heard.
Think of church bells, the end of recess. No fire
extinguisher, no smoke alarm to beep for consolation.
We think that everything that burns was meant to be
consumed first. Food instead of injustice. Water
instead of intolerance. Imagine the flames spreading
like una sad niña learning to make her first bed,

pressing her palms against a bed that won't be hers.
The smoke in her hair crawling over the walls.
She proceeds to grab a copy of the Bible in every
language, since Bible is one of men's primal screams.
If I had to gather those words I've christened
on disaffected ears, all the missing accents
de mi español, I wouldn't have to fear going
back to the country of papier-mâché. America,
when will you stop transiting over the ashes
of our tongues? English is just another word
for deathbed. Once, as a child, I remember running
into my grandmother's house. Someone had set
the house of las maricas on fire. How the tin roof
caved in. How I burned in the brown skin's apathy.

[FONDO/CRIMINAL BACKGROUND CHECK]

...we will employ motion sensors...
        we linger under these highways of empty rhetoric

like intersections that can't be seen no matter how wide the wings
...infrared cameras...unmanned aerial vehicles...

...to prevent illegal crossings...
        our concrete arms are burned from working

entire gospels' worth under the sun. or running from fumes
...the guard will assist the border patrol by operating

surveillance systems...analyzing intelligence...installing
        in the bathroom—what a horrible joke it is to unlearn

breathing. to hold your nose, after all, because once you existed
fences and vehicle barriers...building patrol roads...

...providing training...
        to yourself. never to them. remember when you unlearned

to walk with your own feet, to speak with your own mouth.
...for many years the government did not have

enough space in our detention facilities to hold them
        that also happened to you? how well we remember

the dates when our dignity was taken from us, the sunlight spilling
while the legal process unfolded...

...they walk across miles of desert in the summer heat
    over the stove, the back of every house your house.

walter benjamin developed the concept of the angel of history
or hide in the back of 18-wheelers to reach our country...

...this creates enormous pressure on our border that walls
    after observing paul klee's painting *angelus novus.*

this is how i see it: el ángel gabriel got stuck working
and patrols alone will not stop...a key part of that system

should be a new identification card for every legal
    an extra shift. on his way to our barrio he got caught up

smelling los pastelitos de piña, which, because of his holy senses,
foreign worker...this card should use biometric technology

such as digital fingerprints to make it tamper-proof...
    still smelled fresh, though they'd been sitting there all day.

la migra shows up and gaby can measure destruction
...I believe that illegal immigrants who have roots in our country

and want to stay should have to pay a meaningful penalty
    only after it's happened. he sees the waitress's quiet trailer

and thinks there's nothing to see. angels work in extremes.
for breaking the law...to pay their taxes...to learn english...

and to work in a job for a number of years...english is also
    hermanos, hermanas, niños, niñas are apprehended,

but the angel is mystified by the flashing lights, since heaven
the key to unlocking the opportunity of america...english

allows newcomers to go from picking crops to opening
    shines brightly from its never-ending stupor of contentment.

one apartment's lights won't turn on the same way. a new
a grocery...from cleaning offices to running offices...

from a life of low-paying jobs to a diploma...a career...
    story will move in without a care for backstory. the poet

will need to carve another name on his
*and a home of their own...*arms. the ghosts are out there, shoveling.

Aquí in the Palouse

Veronica Sandoval

Dear Gloria,

Here in the crossroads, with those colorless niños who pride themselves in not seeing color, who keep complaining that all lives should matter and not just black ones. I am exhausted, tired of being a crossroad. My mestiza consciousness isn't healing the split between me and all the mondados in the Palouse. Yes, la Raza and I still live sin fronteras, surviving the borderlands, but here where they only see rolling hills of wheat fields, pine trees and snow covered mountain tops, no se ve la rajada that divides a culture. Los niños fleeing Central America are bedtime stories of welfare parasites and pandemic disease bombs on pause. Se cansa uno of kicking with both feet, and when we pour out the images in our heads for the changes we wish to see, administrators pat us kindly and congratulate us on being so articulate. But all is not hopeless, we keep finding each other here, meeting and dancing in the face of it all. And do not worry Prieta, we remain on both shores, through serpent and eagle eyes, watchando y aprendendo, surviving being a crossroad.

Forever your chola

Water Dream at the Border

Carmen Calatayud

After photograph by Delilah Montoya,
Desire Lines, Baboquivari Peak, AZ
2004, printed 2008, ink-jet print

1.
Dream: A saint with a white guayabera
unloads jugs to dot the desert,
water to ease swelling tongues.

2.
He walks for wandering people,
leaves bottles for thirsty women
in this burnt coral sunset land:
Two countries so close the border
evaporates at night.

3.
Filled plastic jugs hidden behind
jumping cholla in this vista of hope.

4.
Awake: The monsters of fire will come
for you, gun you down under
a moon of ginger flames,
just as your whispers begin to rise.

5.
This borderland named many times,
stolen and taken back again.
The saguaros refuse to fight,
stretch into glitter-blue sky as
white heat feeds the ground.

6.
We chant for survival.
Ravens fly overhead,
offer ebony rings of faith.

7.
If no one knows us
our bones will still mingle
with this dry earth.
They will hiss our names
in the wind.

OUR HIEROGLYPHICS

Juan Morales

After "Placa/Roll Call" by Chaz Bojórquez

The canvas holds the alphabet
of people tagging where the city hurts,
meeting in cholo calligraphy.

The faded black
from an extinct spray can makes
blunt A's, the O's and D's

that could be triangles,

the smeared curves
in the E's and Z's and N's.

We can see future aliens unlocking
the letters but will they know
the embedded names

of the aliens today
that hide in the open
and in the slow invasion of two

languages locked in
the crash of ferocious gridlock?
We must now speak

with the hiss of paint
disrespecting walls in hieroglyphics
that stain and remake our home turf.

Keep On Crossin' Manifesto

Victor Payan

When in the course of human events it becomes necessary to cross borders of political, social, linguistic, cultural, economic, and technological construction... we will cross. For long before there were borders, there were crossers. We are the proud sons and daughters of these crossers, and we hold that crossing is a basic human right. Furthermore, we hold this right to be in-illegal alienable.

Artificial borders of body and mind and spirit must be crossed off the list. For every star-crossed, cross-bearing, cross-platform, cross-dressing, cross-country, cross-walker at the crossroads of culture, the time has come to cross.

We are living in a time when a truckload of toxic waste has more rights to cross than a human being. Wherever and whenever this is the case, we will cross.

Our crossing will be a sign to other crossers that the time has come to cross. We will cross at intersections. Anywhere we cross will become an intersection by the act of our crossing. We will look both ways before crossing, and then, with the positive momentum of humanity, we will cross.

We will cross into other manifestos. These include but are not limited to the Prague Manifesto for Esperanto, the Russell-Einstein Manifesto against nuclear war, the Roxy Music song "Manifesto," the Universal Declaration of Human Rights, the Plan of Delano, the Plan Espiritual de Aztlán, and any other plans, declarations or manifestos that encourage, promote, and reward crossing.

When the border expands, we contract. And when the border contracts, we expand. And when it is time to cross, we will cross all by ourselves.

Wherever there are tired, huddled masses yearning to breathe free, we will cross.

Wherever there's a cop beatin' up a guy, we will cross.

As Martin Luther King wrote from the injustice stained confines of a Birmingham jail: "We are caught in an inescapable network of mutuality, tied in a single garment of destiny."

By wearing this patch, we declare that our garment be counted as a piece from Dr. King's "single garment of destiny."

And to ensure that the sun and moon continue to shine on the smiling faces of the free, we will keep on crossing.

Este Puño Sí Se Ve/Dispatches from Barbed Wire

Abigail Carl-Klassen

Va caer, va caer, este muro va caer

Mujeres Obreras
*Border Wall Protest, Anapra, Chihuahua/Sunland Park, New
Mexico, 2008*

Beneath the iron sky
Mexican children kick their soccer ball across,
run after it, entering the U.S.

Gloria Anzaldúa
Borderlands/La Frontera

They still built the wall. Even though we marched downtown,
jackets and ties peering down from high rises as we shouted,
¡Muro, no. Pueblo sí! After we shut down Paisano, horns
pressed, sage smoke rising, matachines barefoot and rattling.
After we sipped sangre de Cristo through chain links year
after year on Día de los Muertos. After our mayors declared,
¡Ya Basta! San Diego to Brownsville. After ámas pushed
strollers from Douglas to San Elizario. After comadres
from Mujer Obrera, striking hungry, cuffed themselves to
the White House gates and chanted, ¡Obama escucha, estamos
en la lucha! After Red Fronteriza. Hands across the Border.
Via Campesina. Centro Sin Fronteras. Las Americas. Project
Vida. Annunciation House. Border Interfaith. No More Deaths.
DMRS. MEChA. ACLU. Paso Del Norte Civil Rights Center.
Café Mayapan. UTEP Feminists. Unitarians. Low-Rider Kings.
Danza Azteca. Aoy, Guillen and Bowie. Committee for Labor
Justice. The Brown Berets. And even The Sierra Club. Got
together. After every editorial, town hall meeting, and referendum.
After every interview on public television and radio. After every
headline splashed across The *El Paso Times* and *El Diario*.
After every deposition. Every panel. Every conference. Every
prayer service, rosary, and candle. Every documentary filmed
and screened. Every art show and open mic. After every Libro-
traficante underground library and rally. After every fundraising
plato de enchiladas, gorditas, tamales, y pozole. After every

direct action. No rocks, just crosses painted with the names
of the fallen. After every Know Your Rights presentation. After
every housing, tutoring and counseling referral. After every
letter trashed by every congressman and senator. Except for
Beto, who stood in the center of the Bridge of the Americas,
sporting his The Border Makes America Great trucker cap.
After every Donald Trump piñata was bought and smashed.
After the Curandera told us through barbed wire that Lucha is
not just protest, but also pachanga. After the afternoon
we decided to play volleyball, protestors turned into pick-up
teams on each side of the border. The fence, our net, ball
lofting, quiet taps, save the occasional spike and slide in the
sand, laughing above the Migra's megaphone behind us. Cease
and desist. We're still here. In protest. In pachanga. Fists raised.

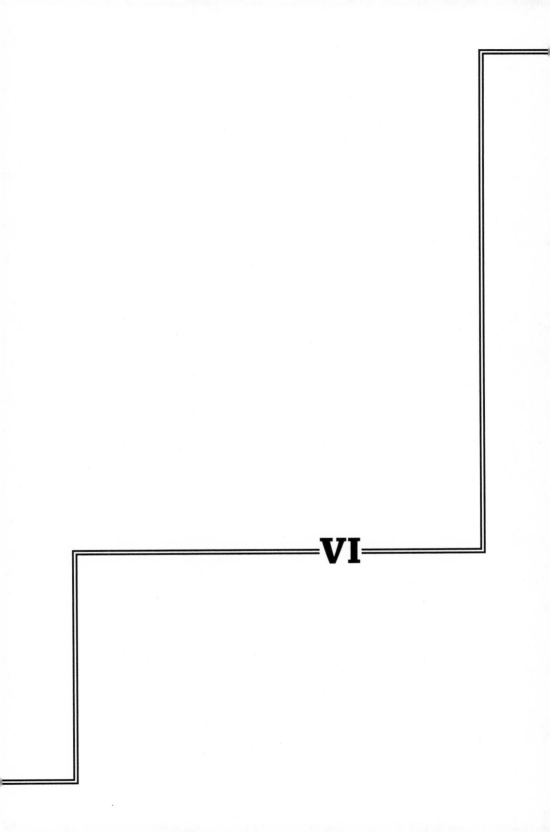

VI

my body is all memory ————————

Sarah A. Chavez

for Gloria Anzaldúa

my body is stone and grit
my body irrigated lawn
my body the rind of an orange

my body is what she made me:
her hands cupped to form breasts, she sliced
a sliver of her tongue and sewed it within
the line she drew at the bottom of my face
which she split with her thumbs to open.
when the dark stitches of saliva fused
tongue to frenulum, she placed her mouth
over my own and her tongue showed
my tongue how to dance, how to touch
its tip behind new teeth, to make T and L
sounds: touch, take, longing, love.

I am a half-formed malcontent, left
in a hut to figure out the rest – how
to mold legs from shifting sand, carve toes
from rock, braid dandelion weeds for hair.
I thought for years she was responsible
for me, but after begging for help, crying
something pitiful and nothing happens
and nothing happens, I realized
I am my own creation, my own
sweet nightmare.

Some of Us Understand the Reason for the Drought

Rachel McKibbens

once they've rid their bodies

    of an impossible country

become flatbed livestock   in migration

    you coin them not of this earth

beings of neither flesh nor light

/ / /

When I was small   I saw men & women—

    soft terrestrial bodies—bent in the field

a mile from the strawberry stand

    in ninety-five degree heat   one hundred

one hundred & three

    I wanted my father to stop the car

to gobble each sunlit jewel

    my mouth luminous, bleeding seeds

NO

    he'd say, sharp / as if their sweat contagious

/ / /

Only once did the woman at the taquería

    speak to me (in audible hieroglyphics)

I knew it was something mine

>   but not mine.

No habla español   my proud father said

>   my silence a thorn shoved

hard into her lip

/ / /

>   When my great-grandparents came

from Guanajuato, they wore

>   no disguises

Manuela vibrant in a handmade dress

>   Pedro (my father's namesake)

in a silent gentleman's hat

>   Did they also imagine becoming ghosts

like I have / like I do

>   boneless satellites in lace   swaying

above their children's heads?

>   If no child of mine

becomes a poet

>   will the absence of this tongue

shimmer like betrayal in their mouths?

inheritance

jo reyes-boitel

I never fully invited the ghost
carried from generation to generation
like an inheritance

that gift serving no one,
that says I must act a certain way
based on the degree my hips curved out
when I turned twelve,
       the gift that relegated me to the indoors
while my brother was thrown outside.

before my period I was hip to hip with my father,
our hands in the truck engine, watering the grass and trees,
or buying a paper bag's worth of chicles and a big red
when we went on errands.

The wilderness of my home's backyard,
the way I knew to rest when the sun warmed the part in my hair.
Eat something, rest, the return again to that green space.
A sun that followed me from sunup to sundown.

Suddenly, my dad's changed.
His face pained. And when I went out
he sent me, over and over again, into the house
to help my mother.

She was happy for the company.

The kitchen was mom's space.

The only sun coming from a tiny window
above the sink.
       An evening sun
always a little cold by the time it met my face,
threw its paleness across the floor tiles.
I claimed a different sun.

My daughter may be the first generation of women of color with freedom assumed. Freedom is never easily attained but she has access to it.

I have worked on making each word possible. Of fully carrying those words within my body. I carry my mother's burdens, am here to decipher them, remove the shackles of gender, class, ethnicity. Struggle is internal, of waiting to give freely, but the expectation of giving a weight impossible to carry.

More than one hundred muscles
    from lungs to lips
must unite
    to pull words
    from our minds

        give each letter its own spirit.

Think of that   cadence
    like frogs singing
    on cool spring evenings
        searching for the one
   who needs that very song
        ruminating in their thoughts.

Think of that   struggle
    in living within another's rhythm
of pulling meter, turning it on its head
creating a new frequency of sound

the work required in crafting
    intent within each
        combination
the next time
   you
      say
          something

without promise.

Mujeres

Adela Najarro

Yo soy Adelita the third, the third
Adela in a backward line
of women before memory and photographs:
Mitadela or Tía Pinita rocking away
a hot afternoon in León, or it could be Managua.
I don't know. Todo se confunde.
It's not only me; we all contribute
to erasure: ¿Qué han hecho las mujeres,
las latinas, mejicanas, dominicanas,
puertorriqueñas, y sí también las nicaragüenses?
Todas ocultadas in this US
culture, in this version of history,
in these times of economic chaotic splendor.
To forget your mother's birthday
is to be una gran hija mala,
but of course I must take note
de todas esas mujeres de mi vida y del pasado.
Una después de otra contribuyendo,
haciendo, criando nuestras penas,
curando nuestras heridas, amándonos
por el resto de nuestras vidas.
I carry many names as daughter,
la hija de Juanita, Lela, Mitadela, y Tía Pinita.
A daughter de todas las planchadoras,
lavanderas, maestras y damas de casa
watching telenovelas on Univision wondering
if María Dolores will ever be found
hiding in a convent.
Does being a woman have to entail
una vida de sufrimiento?
I try to swing out from the shadows,
touch the lowest branch
of a eucalyptus tree, and over the years
have found words at rest in mi pasado y las voces
de las poetas olvidadas

sin recompensación, pero todavía vivas,
the women, the mothers
alive in our hearts.
We look to the East
cada mañana y hambriente
para el sol
comienza la aurora.

Dar a Luz

Elsie Rivas Gómez

I.

Había crecido con la idea que el amor de mi familia was this unconditional thing like earth, abundant and deep, rich and brown, the essential nutrient.

Pero fui equivocada. It's easy to love someone who meets every expectation. Easy to love the American degrees on the wall, the house on a tree-lined street, the man standing there like an *esposo* should, his hands resting on the two *niñas* with fair skin.

For an immigrant family to claim these symbols of the American Dream is really something, isn't it? What's not to love?

II.

Mami.
What's not to love?

The hint of queerness, the *puta* peeking out from behind my face. Two-faced *mujer* who can love regardless of gender. Bisexual, the word that salted the earth beneath my feet. *¡chas!* Like that.

Visitas con abuelita called off. My goddaughter forbidden from me.

¡Qué Vergüenza!

Nepantlera caught by the throat.

How can it matter at all, *Mami*? You live in San Francisco, where everyone is queer.

Pero no yo. It doesn't matter how perfectly I contorted my spirit to fit the colonizer's mold. The errant kinky hair, the flesh non-conforming, enough to reveal the queer *india* in me.

The imperative to hide, to protect the family. Why tell anyone at all when it is so easy to pass? A history of passing with light skin, with California accents, with ambiguous features. The convenience of invisibility.

But invisibility is its own death.

I will not eat my own tail in an effort to keep others comfortable. I will strike and bite and take what I need to survive, as all *animales* do. Erasure is not my nature; do not mistake my coloring for camouflage. Just because you did not see me at first does not mean I'm not here.

Un año without seeing you, Mami. The girls have grown tall. They ask when you'll visit again, when we will visit you.

We do get phone calls from you – stilted and distant now. As if you are back in El Salvador, or as if I am on Mars. I can barely recognize my own voice when we speak.

Todos llaman when I send the message that I'm pregnant again, this time, with *un hijo*. I amend the soil around my house, scatter coffee grounds and egg shells, spread fresh mulch and manure. I set out the rain barrels, prepare for the torrential rain of El Niño.

If I want to survive, I know I'll have to work it out directly with the clouds, and stones, and worms.

III.

There can be no hiding the queer in me. There are three children whose dark eyes will track my every gesture. Nepantleras each of them, with my arms stretching wide the borderlands for them so that they may have safe crossings, so that their skin never be considered a trespass.

I touch my lover and I am neither woman nor man, just hands, and mouth, and desire. He touches me and his tongue is a flame lighting the oil on my skin. *Chingada,* does it matter how we fuck?

There is a queerness about a mother fucking and being fucked that is particularly troubling to the moral enforcers. A transgression to see the round belly and milk-full breasts bared with lust. Queer to let the milk wash over my skin as I climax. Nepantla moving between woman as sexual and woman as maternal. Nepantla as sexual maternal.

The love of my family of origin may be revealed to be as thin as sandy oil, but within these walls, the family I have chosen and borne, we eat tamales and pupusas with the windows open to the scent of freshly turned earth.

IV.

Nepantla means letting go of my mother and all others who let go of me. I can't make her love a queer daughter the way she used to love a straight one. Nepantla means holding space for those coming up alongside me and after me.

Nepantla means that even when I fuck a man, it is still queer. The queer is me, not his desire for me. Nepantla means floating in the prenatal space where anything is possible. The placental earth connecting and sustaining all of us who dare to speak our true names.

Where love is rescinded, we will restore the dark earth for ourselves. We will sow our own hybrid seeds. They will flower the color of blood and bear a fruit that never dies.

Photograph of "Woman in Red Dress, Sunflowers, Sitting With Blanket" Lupe Mendez

Oígame, doña, ¿y esos mirasoles? ¿a cuanto los vende? Ándale, véndemelas ¿no? Y la cobija también, que las líneas en negro y blanco remind me of a tent entrance to a circus at the edge of a field, a field in Tlajamulco, so straight, so propped up, parece capa, eres majestad con esa capa, at the edge of you y los mirasoles, they grow out of you right now, you grow out of the wall, you grow into the sky, your trenzas are long, stem stocks tied in bright yellow orange, you grow into the clouds, the white ones that sit next to you, your hair Doña, enrollado en rayos de sol, amarillo profundo, véndeme su pelo, los rayos, ándale, doña, no sea mala, véndemelas ¿no? No, no sus ojos, ni su respiro, pero las flores, I am sorry, I should have complimented you on your purple, tu rosada, tu morada, your pink vestido, lleno de lunares, la cobija lleno de rayas en los rayos del sol, el sol, el sol que la cubre en un fulgor, que la cubre, que el sol extiende su boca y bese su piel, un beso en su frente, que brille, que brille, que brille. Perdón, doña, véndeme su tiempo, su silencio, su espacio en la pared, sus pies que no puedo ver, sus manos que son mirasoles, hecho de nubes, hecho de rostro, hecho de paz, de paz, de paz, mejor, la dejo doña, la dejo, la dejo, solita, mirasol, en paz.

In the fields I walked to where you hummed

T. Sarmina

I know we walked here together
me in your belly,
walking along your veins like rivers,
sliding down the slopes of your heart,
peeking into the caves where
you held and hold everything
I walked inside you
before I walked out of you
and that is why I was born
so fast

I've climbed the bones of the cage
you hold yourself in
it was the first playground
I learned to fall in
I kept warm in the tissues
of your muscles, hard in places,
torn in others,
I walked along your veins, past
your heart on my map,
sat in your throat to hear you
hum as you picked oranges and grapes

Messenger Hornets

Shauna Osborn

I have dropped my eyes into slits
seen my apartment filled with
the brown bodies of my maternal ancestors
folded like layers of dulce barato
that hard-ass striped ribbon candy
between the bookshelves & ragged-edged posters
covering the dirty white cement walls.

They will not go away.

Mis madres balance in their hands
what remains of their bloodied wombs
their bodies stained & beaten. I recognize their faces
find gaping holes & missing jawbones
find hands & feet broken decades before.
Some gnaw on their own hair to tell our
tribe they have not forgotten our grieving rites.
They thump me on the forehead to get my attention
to force my eyes to follow their line of vision.

Many times I've tried to overlook them
to forget that they have searched years to
find me hiding from them under this Anglican skin.
I've pretended not to understand their tongues &
refused their silence as well. I've tired of the stings
their messenger hornets have left in my neck, legs, arms, & palm.
I've tired of navigating left & right through their numbers to get to the
bathroom or the front door. I've tired of the heavy chill they leave in the air
surrounding my bed, of waking both hands tightened into fists all
bloody, scratched, my jaw sore from constant teeth grinding
the smells of earth & bitter roots they leave in my kitchen
all the lemons they leave tiny, brown, & dry.

I have to write them out of my office
off my couch
into existence here on the page.
I have to find them a resting place that will
release their rage somewhere it's needed
somewhere it can do some good.

rearranging the bones

Marie Varghese

mama, it's funny how i unearth
verses of my life
for an audience of strangers
never for you.
entrails of my secrets
harden like clay soil
my mouth consumes the stillness
crafting absence for language.

i know you never asked
to birth a dyke for a daughter
so i bury bittersweet
beneath a hungry crucifix.
i settle for a crowd
full of silences between us.

we brown girls don't bruise so easy, mama.
earning silver strands
that crown our hair
sometimes we swallow
our own desires for survival.

mama, i walk with your shakti in my bones
you taught me my heart
is entangled with muscles
of every brown woman
that came before me

but stillborn whispers choke the chords
until i free my lungs
fierce fists juxtaposed against the sky
i'll unearth my secrets for multitudes
instead of you.

i am not drawing out
the skeletons of our closets
i am only rearranging the bones.

I Went to Pray My Grandmother's Prayer

Allen Baros

> La facultad is the capacity to see in surface phenomena the meaning of deeper
> realities, to see the deep structure below the surface. It is an instant "sensing,"
> a quick perception arrived at without conscious reasoning [...] The one
> possessing this sensitivity is excruciatingly alive.
>
> **Gloria Anzaldúa**
> *Definition of la facultad, "Entering into the Serpent"*

I never leave the borderlands. Not really. I'm not sure if that's an inspiring or
disheartening thing to write, but it is more than a little true. The borderlands
are a place where things stop making sense. Where one world makes demands
for meaning on individuals who mean something on their own make meaning
differently in different worlds.

I know that not only am I of the borderlands, but that I carry the borderlands
with me. I know that when I walk into a room I make them the borderlands.
From where I stand, I make and unmake and remake meaning as I see and cross
over and stop stumbling at borders that I know are there to create meaning of
their own. Truth becomes something to question. Questions start to make up a
questionable landscape made clear only through violence and disruption. Only
the contradictions are clearly defined.

How do you explain that to someone? The space between where you are in the
borderlands, on a thin edge of barbed wire, and where someone stands, or sits,
in comfort beyond?

I walked into a cathedral, a big one in the heart of Seattle. The city I moved to when
I left Albuquerque. It's beautiful, white and laced with gold, and I know there is
a lovely white statue of the Virgin holding the baby Jesus and crowned queen of
heaven just around the side looking over a stone waterway that is part of a fountain.

I went in and looked for the bowl of holy water and felt silly.

"Why do I still cross myself?" I asked.

Grandma's not here to scold me for not doing it, I think to myself. Nobody is
watching me, in fact there are really only a few people in this big church today.

I look at the doorway for a bowl of holy water and do not find it. Turning around I see a huge bowl made of marble in the middle of the walkway. It also is a flowing fountain and I giggle at how much more fancy this place is compared to the little St. Edwin's Church I went to as a kid. I walk past the pews and notice the lavish cross in the center of the church. It's a strange (at least to me) set up, with the altar in the center like theater in the round.

Where do I genuflect?

Why do I still genuflect? Who am I bowing to?

My knee touches the ground and I cross myself again and I hear in my head, just like when I was in third grade, Grandma Lottie say "Mira, mi 'jito. He kneels and crosses himself just like they did in the old days."

Something feels better when I think of that. I think it's because for a moment, I make sense in this space.

That's really my problem. This place is beautiful, and while it is very different from the church I went to as a kid, the church I stopped going to but to talk to a small statue of the Virgin of Guadalupe, it seems all of a piece. Aside from me, it makes sense.

Well, for a moment it did. Standing up, I realize I didn't come to this church for anything it has to offer. I feel like I went into the mall for the air conditioning or a park for sex. Feeling dirty and for some reason excited, afraid someone will catch me and figure me out. I don't want to be figured out.

I see a woman at a small desk near the small shrine to the Virgin. She has pamphlets with pictures of the church on them in front of her and they're arranged neatly along the edges of the small desk. She's new, and so is her desk. I've come here before and I never saw her there. I think it's strange.

"Can I help you?"

STOP. I stopped right there.

You don't ask something like that,

I wanted to shout, but in my mind both of my grandmothers mutter something under their breath about white people not knowing any better. It makes me want to laugh, but I try not to giggle here in the shadowy hallway of this church.

She looked like she was helpful. Insistently and aggressively helpful. Determined to be helpful. She helpfuled right at me in fact, asking again if she could help me.

I mumbled something about finding my way and "just here to talk to the Virgin." She motioned toward the shrine and pointed to the little slot on the way telling me that the suggested donation was a dollar per candle.

Not far from there I saw flowers, starting to fade here in the afternoon, and I thought *you should have brought some flowers. Grandma always did. You like picking them out.*

"Where do I leave flowers?" I ask, and she looks at me as though she doesn't understand.

"For the Virgin." I continue. "I wanted to bring flowers; where do I leave them?"

"I think they take care of that." She says. "I know that they do that kind of thing at St. Edward's, where the." She stops for a moment. "In South Seattle." She finishes.

I hope that she wasn't going to say *where the Mexicans go,* because I want something better than that in my life today, but I'm almost sure it was what she meant to say.

"Yeah, it's what we did where I grew up." I tell her. I leave out that I just used to like bringing gifts to the Virgin of Guadalupe with my Grandmas, or going with either of them to light candles for her.

"No, I think they take care of that here." She continues, "And if they didn't, I couldn't even imagine the kinds of flowers that people might bring." She laughs and I, somewhat lost for words say,

"Yeah, I'm sure." Trying to sound good-natured though I don't know why.

I walk past her and I feel her watching me.

I stood in the thin hallway lit by thin candles all clustered around the Virgin. Five years here in Seattle and this still puts me off each time I come. The Virgin is dressed in gold here, and not green. She wears a crown of gold, but there is no halo of light around her head. Her skin is ivory, not brown, and when I kneel before her, I smell flowers, but not roses.

I feel a familiar fear in me as I think *it won't be the same.*

I push it back. I just need to talk. Not to the statue of a white woman dressed in gold but to a line just in between what I know and what I don't totally understand. Past the statue, where I can't touch but where I can feel and if I try hard, where I can sometimes see. I ignore her golden gown.

Think past this. Move past it. In between what is here and what I've brought here.

I just wish I could say what it is, and why I brought it—why I bring it.

On my knees I start to pray. Not the Lord's Prayer but my grandma's.

> Remember, O most gracious Virgin Mary,
> That never was it known that anyone who fled to your protection,
> Implored your help or sought your intercession,
> Was left unaided.

I know the words. Learned them by rote. And I'm not there in the small hall with the ivory woman garbed in gold, watched over by unfamiliar eyes with expectations formed to fit a clean-cut white cathedral in the heart of a West Coast city.

I slip past that border,

> Inspired by this confidence, I fly unto thee,
> O Virgin of Virgins, my mother; to thee do I come,
> Before thee I stand, sinful and sorrowful.

The words seem strange, like a touch without a body or warmth without a fire. I know what they mean but I know that they mean something else now when I say them, when I remember my grandmother saying them.

In bed at my Grandma Sara's house and I'm eight again. She has a rosary out, a small one with green beads, and there is a small prayer card above the bed we share when I stay over, and a picture of the Virgin of Guadalupe looks out from it.

> O Mother of the Word Incarnate,
> Despise not my petitions,
> But in thy mercy hear and answer me.

She finishes and I finish and I hear her voice and my own when I whisper, "Amen."

She recites those words, those strange words that I know cannot be hers because she doesn't talk that way. Because they leave her mouth dry. I know because she says the words like she talks when she needs to sound professional. The way she talks to white people. Licking the top of her mouth and smacking, quietly and precisely before she speaks.

When she says "or sought your intercession, was left unaided" she says it with meaning. With meaning that she had found and put into those words. I don't know what she means when she says it but I knew, for my grandma, saying the words was important. I knew for her, they meant more than words could mean on their own. Words made all her own with meaning from deep inside her and shared there with me and the Virgin. I always thought it was magic.

I would lay in bed with her and listen to those words and know that nothing bad could happen now. I was wrapped in something powerful, thick, and soft, like my Grandma's arms.

I kneel in a church, not speaking to any god, not sure if there is one.

But confident now that I can speak to a statue of a woman who is not the Virgin of Guadalupe, speaking, all the while to a picture of the Virgin of Guadalupe beyond the borders of that golden gown and this white stone cathedral.

Speaking all the time to my grandma who took care of me and let me know that I could fly to her and be inspired to confidence, never unaided, and always loved. I smell roses somewhere beyond where I can touch and between what I am and what I hope to be.

I understand what I'm doing here now.

In this shrine, between the stares of these two white women who are not my grandmothers, who are not the Virgin of Guadalupe and Juan Diego, who are not Coatlicue come again, for a moment, a flash, I know what I am doing. I find no why or reason to it, but I know what I am doing.

In between those things, as I lose track of what could mean what, I find myself dreaming. I am dreaming!

Someone who loves me watches me pray, watches me smell the roses that are not there and that I dream are everywhere. I don't dream that my prayers are answered, I don't know what that would mean. I dream that my grandma's words are wrapped around me and reaching out to make the world as I dream it. Better, though I don't know what that means outside of my dream. I feel hope, bright and burning like a new sun. In the light of that sun, I imagine how that world could be.

Imagine a world where my brother succeeds at everything. Where my sister is happy and untroubled, where my partner achieves great things. Where nobody stumbles over road blocks or their own two feet.

I imagine a world where I'm very happy and those I love are happy too. Happy in ways that I can't find words to describe. A world in which everyone I love—family and friends—live wonderful happiness. I let it overwhelm me and wash over me until I know the world I'm imagining is bigger and grander than I can understand. Until what I imagine became a dream again, undefined and only half understood.

And it's alive for a moment, and shining, burning, blazing, pouring all around me and in me and touching everyone.

And then I'm back, kneeling before the ivory white Virgin in her golden gown. Under the watchful eyes of someone at a desk taking care that I do not leave those unimaginable flowers at the feet of our lady in gold.

I realize what I do there, in the borderlands of consciousness between what I appear to be and what I am. Between what is here and what I carry with me. I go there to imagine.

I don't care that that world I dreamed of only exists in a flash, in my mind, in a breath of half-dreamt roses. It doesn't matter that it all starts in a small bed in a dark adobe house, with the smell of cigarettes and black coffee mixing with chile and beans from dinner. Out where memories need to be made whole by imagining.

I saw what I do in a dream from beyond where anything makes senses. In the borderlands that I carry with me. And dreaming a world I want gives me hope. Hope to imagine something that takes place not in my dreams or half-imagined memories, but here, where I am now, making and remaking the world in love and hope in the borderlands between what is and what we who love so much want to be.

Xiuhatl[1] ⎯⎯⎯⎯⎯⎯⎯⎯⎯⎯⎯⎯
(becoming turquoise)

Alexis Pauline Gumbs

i.

people say
my grandmother could
bring rain
my grandfather asked for it
in letters from their desert island
my aunt noticed the short rain shower
that ended right before grandma's funeral
and said "see? she's with us."
and besides designing the revolutionary flag
and founding the first mental health association
in the Caribbean
she was also
the founder of the
Anguilla beautification club

accountable to flowers.

ii.

most often
I wear my grandma's
turquoise art deco necklace
because it opens my heart
because it is heavy and grounding
because what would she say
did it remind her of Rendezvous Bay in Anguilla
(the place she decided to stay)

iii.

turquoise develops
when copper and iron and calcites
get transformed by rain

---

1   In the Nahuatl language "the turquoise waters of paradise."

are they blue for the sun
that seems to have left them
or blue for the water again

iv.

my name is salt
my name is sand
i am shaped by
my grandmother's hand

v.

my grandmother was afraid of heights
and she flew around the world
and her granddaughter is analog itinerant
a luddite on a digital twirl

vi.

in Mexico jade was abundant
but turquoise was hard to find
but turquoise was rarely mined
but the gods loved it and wanted
infinite mosaics so the people
sought and climbed
so the pilgrimage was refined
grandma you are on my mind

vii.

Tlaloc is the Aztec god of rain
ultimately he decides
if you eat sand or drink salvation
father to whom invites the tides
his first wife
was the goddess of flowers
he is holding up the sky
at its four sides
so it doesn't fall
on the daydreamers
who look up
or google
for hours

viii.

and Tlaloc has grandchildren too
whom he loves more than anyone else
one breaks his skin to feed the masses
one gives up her whole self
every year
right at the neck

ix.

did my grandmother find this necklace
far from its rebirth home
or did she travel to another desert
to test her portable magic

x.

where Tlaloc lives it is luscious
endless verdant spring
and my grandmother squints and laughs
still doing her thing

xi.

and she rises with the ocean when it sings
and she coughs with the wind when it blows
and she brailles her name in the dirt
she is the reason that anyone grows

xii.

i am wearing her necklace
i can do anything
i know

Translation ──────────────

Ysabel Y. González

Tio Rufino was buried in the Bronx, New York. In an alternate universe, here is how his funeral might have looked.

We are a trail of hummingbirds
following nectar's smell,
the flower opens
farther down the road,
Tio Rufino's house buried
in mountain green in Puerto Rico.
We find his corpse sweet—
sticky like guava paste
melting on our tongues
and we buzz
with rosaries,
praise Tio Rufino's body
like a healed wound.

When my cry escapes
my throat
cuatros and accordions play
like ointment on a burn;

novena to triumph
Tio's way to heaven.
We'll sip café, rich chocolate
while singers fill their chords
with folksong notes
slicing their way
through island heat
cooling us like a swing
from a machete
at the tops of bamboo.

Our sendoff has favors:
queso blanco and bread,
nine jubilant nights
brimming with coquí chants

A party in Puerto Rico
for a man that lived—Ay, Rufino!
you can almost see his head
nodding to the music.
Watch him grooving,
his hand making its way to his hip,
feet shuffling against the casket.
It's his time to dance again;
he's saying to Mother God:
baile, baile
It's our time to dance again
baile, baile

and he rocks oak wood with his elbows
cement underneath pounding to the beat

And now you're home Tio
the rooster cocks his head in salute,
Tia Fela swoons to the tune.
Everybody is up from their seats
arms cheering upward,
eyes wait for that soft pink sun
to rise like rose in an infant's cheek
because captions aren't needed
for this kind of celebration.

VII

At Night My Body Splits and Splits

Sarah A. Chavez

At night, the white half and the brown half
half. The white male quarter and white
female quarter lick each other's cheeks
before moving in opposite directions.

He to a bro bar on the north side of town
where many white men will drink
their weight in Budweisers and watch brown
men's bodies collide, ACLs and hamstrings
tear, contusions form, concussions born
from the crack of helmet on helmet.
They slap their white palms together and cheer.

The white female quarter slips milky legs
through a short pleated skirt, ties symmetrical
bows in the clean white laces of clean white
Keds and hails a cab to the tennis courts.
Under the floodlights, she marvels at the elegance
of her own play: how effortless smooth
her swing, how the other white women sweat.

The brown male quarter throws his laundry
at the brown female quarter and slaps
her ass on his way out the door, saying,
Don't come back knocked up.

He hitches a ride on the back of a truck
out to the fields where the moon is as large
as the working man's anger and the stars
are pricks of light in the tarp of sky. He meets
his compadres who talk politics and smoke *mota.*
After they are good and high, cans of Coors
littering the rows of cracking dirt, they whisper
how much love they carry for one another.

The brown female quarter kicks the bag
of laundry out of her way, steps into four-inch

red, strapless heels, locks the door, and goes dancing:
mambos and salsas, cha cha chas and flamenco.
She goes to many clubs and at each one the bright
flair of flower petal skirt lifts and lilts to the beat
of brown hands on a drum, her hips following
the sonar of brown voices.

In predawn twilight, each quarter returns
stumbling back, part drunk, stretching their arms
overhead in exaggerated shows of exhaustion.

The white female drapes her arms around the brown
female, pulls her in. They merge, breasts and bones,
hair and skin. The brown male and white male
do the same, first arm to arm, then shoulder
to shoulder, chest and the rest. The beige
male and female crawl under the covers and melt
into this one body and I wake up,
their experiences the union of my perception.

Nocturne for Rattlesnakes and Lechuzas

Joe Jiménez

i.

Anzaldúa once admitted it took her 40 years
"to enter into the serpent, to acknowledge I
have a body."

I used to think I'd never hold 40
years
in my mouth.

She was cutting quelites with her
family. Wild Mexican greens. The ones that
had "outlived the deer's teeth."

Fuck, she can write so beautifully.

When I die, I want to also be buried
in deer's teeth. I want my mouth to fill
gently with sand and lechuzas.

A few times I have thought of laying
my big body beside a deer—.

Near a road.
In a field made of huisache and moon—.

To hold its long breath, to beg its hot
deer-heart to beat slowly
and only for me.

ii.

Tonight, I near 40: and I trace an owl on a
pad, watch a television show where people
make beautiful things
        out of organza and seams.

The owl steadies my hand:
        wing covert, torsus, face-disc—,
        scapulars and steam.
        My wrist believes it is young.
        The control comforts my heartspan,
where it rests.
        The alula, it seems—

but I also want to make beautiful things—.
        Sometimes, I want others to see me
as beautiful, too.
        Not rough, not voracious.
        Not ever wielding the machete of my
body, splitting anyone in two.

        But I don't want to have to lose the
brownness I'm in to obtain it—beauty,
gentleness, flight—.

        My body is full of tunnels.
Hollowness, but not like a bird's.

I'm ashamed for fearing heights,
        so I'd make a really fucked-up bird.

        Sometimes, I think not wanting to
look out the window of a high-rise makes
me less of a man.
        Sometimes, I'm afraid the dim, firm
husk that grows over me makes me more of
one.

iii.

In the anecdote Anzaldúa shares, she is
snake-bitten, she can feel the venom in her
body, and she buries the rattlesnake that
bites her

      "between the rows of cotton." She
says this on page 48.

      She says the earth is a coiled serpent.

And she is immune.
          Often, I wish I, too, could
bury the rattlesnake. Maybe digging
a hole is where my beauty will be found.

But I haven't been in a cotton field in a good
grip of years.

But sometimes I simply want the snake to
enter me, to coil inside me

      and stay.

      Most times, I just wish I could spend
all night digging holes in a field
of huisache
and deer hearts and moon—
      as if anyone could still be immune.

Dawson, NM. 1913

Rachel McKibbens

Night awakens,
or someone's mouth,
& out steps blood
& marrow in a dress.
A long wool thing.
Dead brass watch
on a flat-boned wrist.

With a hiss of braids
coiled atop her head
and infant girl
strapped to her chest,
she arrives.
As whole as a woman can be.

Here she is permitted
the pleasures
of the ordinary:
pale grit of masa
spread quickly
into husks,
the calloused edge
of her husband's hand.

Settling into this
foreign home,
there is no need
to daydream,
no chore interrupted.
Praise be the asylum
of such repetition:
dishes cleaned,
then stacked.
Skirts hemmed,
floors swept.

New Mexican soil
still intact, un-mined,
still something
like a gift.
Her daughter
dreaming in milk,
her gentle husband
not yet charred.

Why, then, would she
notice the crows
gathering like germs
on her porch,
throats
chilling the air
with a cold
death noise?

Regeneration

Minal Hajratwala

migrants
washed / unwashed
clinging to our magic

we walk invisibly
through the spitting could-be
trying to give birth

to haptic bodies — whose? —
of work

of water
of / if pure light

form

Miguel M. Morales

I struggle to form thoughts
about my shape, my
landscape, my
climate, my
underrated form.

Queer brown fat words
from my wild tongue fail
to convince me that my
bulky frame deserves the same
ornate framing as yours.

Averting eyes drag across
my mass pulling at me
pressing me to pull at my
rumpled sleeves and my
delinquent collar.
I pull up my slumping pants
and pull down my
insurgent shirt.

I pull myself together,
pull *all* myself together,
for your comfort
remembering always
to remain covered
—unexplored shores.

In the marrow of my silence
free from the constraints
of the body,
free from the struggle
with my own hands
and with my own mind,

nepantla nourishes me
shaping thoughts

about my shape,
about my (id)entity.

My form takes words
as my words take form.

VIII

where the wild tongues are

Karla Cordero

beyond caged teeth. between raised fist
& beating heart. beasting with the wolves.
stands straight for the bow. learns to arrow.
wears bullet as its coat. boils in the blood
of its motherland. buried under snake skin.
becomes brick on the back of resistance.
beats the earth. swallows the bees. blesses
the honey. & savors the bones of bliss.

The Waters de Mi Nombre

Xochitl-Julisa Bermejo

"Jaque-a-tail? Is Jaque-a-tail here?" It was my first day of t-ball, and I was standing in a green field with an oversized glove sitting on the wrong hand.

"Jaque-a-tail?" the tall, shaggy-haired dad called out again, and I remember thinking, *That name is weird. Who has that name?*

"X-O-C-H— "

"That's me!" I said, admitting to being the owner of "Jaque-a-tail."

At five and in my first year of school, this was only the beginning of many years of new teachers, coaches, and classmates. By the time I was in junior high, I took to stopping the teacher at the front of the classroom as soon as I saw her slim face contort.

"I'm right here!" I'd say. "I'm SO-chee," and the teacher would exhale in appreciation of my save.

Over the years, I got accustomed to introducing myself as "SO-chee like that's so cheesy," in hopes of overstepping awkward pronunciations such as X-O-chitel, Exauchitel, and Jaque-a-tail. But even with the overly simplistic pronunciation, I still got the ever annoying SO-shee, or the absolutely intolerable ZO-shee. I said "SO-chee" because if I introduced myself as Xochitl, well-meaning people tended to say "SO-cheal" or "SO-chill like you're so chill," and that was more than I could handle. So I dubbed myself "SO-chee" for most of my young life.

At 16, I met a cute boy with shiny, blond hair that draped over shaved sides and tasseled just above his prep school uniform collar. He was a year ahead of me in school and the lead singer in a garage band with other boys from his class. As soon as he met me, he fell in love with my name. I like to pretend he fell in love with me, but honestly, it was just my name.

We were standing under the walkway awning next to the library during a short break. The sun was shining on us and our reflections showed in the library's wall of glass windows.

"This is SO-chee." His bandmate introduced us.

"So-CHI!" the blond boy said excitedly. "So-CHI? Like you have the qi? That is so QI!"

His religion teacher earlier in the day had told his class a story about how he had learned to harness his qi and that in harnessing his qi he was able to stop himself from killing a man with his bare hands (or something like that).

The boy loved my name so much that he wrote a song about it with his bandmates. Legend goes that he always wanted to write a song with the title, "If My Amp Had Wheels," and after he met me he was inspired to write it. The chorus went, "Sochi, Sochi, I'm so glad you are so she," and I loved it! Who wouldn't want to be the inspiration for a song, or be the bearer of the name that was an inspiration for a song?

I loved it so much that I bought their $3 demo tape and played it over and over. I played it for anyone who would listen. One afternoon, I played it for my cousins on my mom's stereo. It was one of those multi-layered, robot-like stereo systems with a turntable at the top and levers for treble and base blinking through its midsection. I slapped in the tape and punched play. The song scratchily released from the two speaker towers.

I started dancing around the living room and singing along: "If my amps had wheels, I would go real fast, and if my amp had speakers, then we'd really have a blast. Haaaaaaave a blast! YEAH!"

My cousins sat on the couch unimpressed.

"Don't worry. It's coming up right now. You'll see," I assured them.

The chorus hit, and they instantly started laughing.

"What's so funny?" I asked. "Don't you like it?"

"No," my cousin Monique said. "It's weird."

"Weird. What do you mean?"

"Well, who is 'sOH-chee?'" She over accentuated the O like a California surfer, like Keanu Reeves exclaiming, "Oh, shit!"

"That's me!" I said, "The song is about me!" I lied.

"That's not your name," Monique said.

I was confused.

"Your name is Xochitl, Xoch. These white boys are saying your name all wrong." Never had I noticed that my family pronounced my name differently than I did. But she was right. My entire family called me either "Sau-chil" or "Sau-chi," and never did they use the full California sun "Oh" or the "CHEE" like that's so cheesy. It was something softer. I had spent the last 10 years so fiercely battling the X-O-chitels and Jaque-a-tails, that I couldn't hear the quieter spaces of my own name.

When I was little I hated my name and wished it was Heather like feather. Like '80s feathered hair, something light and easy, and nothing like the kinks and knots of Xochitl. But when I was twenty-two I traveled to Mexico City with my mom to see Pope John Paul II canonize Juan Diego. After the ceremony, she rushed me into a cab and instructed the cab driver to take us 45 minutes out of the city to Xochimilco even though we had been up since 4 AM. Once there, we climbed into one of the many rainbow gondolas crowned with over-sized names like "Teresita" and "Gabriela." As we drifted along the flower waterways, I caught my name etched into the side of a teal wooden canoe. At Teotihuacan, I stood at the base of a stone pyramid and found red and green painted flowers. The sign next to it read, "Xochitl: flower." In the Museo de Antropología, I encountered Xochitl carved at the top of the behemoth stone Aztec calendar, the 20th day. I began to realize that Xochitl wasn't so strange. Xochitl was history. Xochitl was stone. Xochitl was blooming.

I am a first generation Chicana, and I didn't grow up speaking Spanish, unless it was broken words to my grandmother like, "Quiero cornflais, grandma. Por favor!" or to fold my hands and bow my head after a meal she served me to say, "Gracias ha dios," only to slyly add, "y gracias ha Grandma," which she always grimaced at disapprovingly. My parents spoke to me in Spanish, "¿Saludaste a tu tía?" and I would reply, "Yes, I said hi when I walked in." We might be walking around a store, and my father would order, "Amarate los zapatos," and I'd bend down to tie my loose laces. If my mother called from another room and I yelled out, "What?" I was certain to hear, "No dices, 'Wha?' Dices, '¿Manda Usted?'" Spanish words were always a part of my home floating in the air like Vicente Fernandez croons or the spice of roasting chiles picking at the throat.

Spanish was intimate, spoken between us, in the home, but when we are not careful, our names become public and no longer belong to us.

Though I grew up hearing Spanish every day, I also grew up saying my last name as "Ber-MAY-ho" very much like I said "SO-chee." I would continue saying "Ber-MAY-ho" well into my thirties without thought. That is, until I began writing poetry and building a writing career in L.A., which can include being featured at readings around the city now and again.

At one such reading for a journal's new issue release in Santa Monica, I suddenly became aware of the distance that had grown between my name and me.

The host of the reading, a sheepish brunette, walked up to the microphone and said, "The next writer up has an impressive bio, and we are very excited to have her here. Um…" Suddenly, I saw her face twist and her eyes turn wide as she scanned the audience for me. She was asking for the save, but this time I didn't acquiesce.

"Oh my, if I only knew how to say her name. Um, SO-chit-el-Jewl-isa Ber-may-JO. Oh goodness. I know that's wrong. Oh my…" She went on apologizing for another minute. She talked about how she should have asked first, how she should have known better, how hosting can be so hard.

I wanted her to stop. *You don't know it, that's fine. No one does, but stop. For god's sake! Stop!*

"Well, she can tell you how to say her name, I'm sure. Please welcome, um," and she moved away from the microphone in a mumble with her head down.

I took my cue to walk up and introduce myself, but here's the thing, even I didn't know how to say my own name. I had retrained myself to say Xochitl with its soft edges, and Julisa, my second name, I have always been able to whistle through, and sometimes when I say it I think of my eldest brother Julio. Julio has always been Julio and never Jew-lee-OH. But now there is my last name to add, my last name that I have forever said as "Ber-MAY-ho." I remember once, when I was a kid I heard my middle brother's school friend say our last name properly with the accent, and my youngest brother and I thought he said "pendejo." Bermejo sounds an awful lot like pendejo if you listen just right, so I always said "Ber-MAY-ho."

Standing up at the microphone, instructed to introduce myself because the host didn't know how to say my name, suddenly I was struck with the same problem. Do I say SO-chee Who-Lisa Ber-MAY-ho, or do I say Xochitl-Julisa Bermejo, or do I say Xochitl-Julisa Ber-MAY-ho? The third option felt the most natural, but also the most preposterous. So what did I do?

"Hi everyone! I'm Xochitl-Julisa Ber—" and I backed away from the microphone in a mumble with my head down like a real pendeja.

Xochitl-Julisa Bermejo is a whole lot of name, especially when I write poems about my grandmother in East L.A., and stories from Mexico, and stories from the border. My name and art carry a certain pressure that says I should be able to say my own name with authority, but in that moment I couldn't. And I felt like a fraud.

I've heard it from others too. My own friends have implied as much from time to time. "You don't speak Spanish. Why do you have Spanish in your poems?" Lex asked after a reading she came to in Highland Park. Lex is Spanish, born in Spain, and often tells me I'm saying the wrong word for things like cruda. "We don't use that word," she told me once.

"Lex, I'm from L.A. It's L.A. Spanish, and I do speak it," I said. Her raised eyebrow told me she wasn't so convinced, and sometimes I'm not so convinced either.

Maybe to be uncertain is to be Chican@. Luis J. Rodriguez, in his essay, "How Xican@s Are the Makeweight of Los Angeles's Past, Present, and Future," wrote, "Xican@s are more like water, an ocean or wavering river, slithering like Quetzalcoatl through borders, cultures, labels, races, languages." As a Chicana in Los Angeles, I grew up floating between English and Spanish aimlessly like a leaf in the river, but as I begin to build my writing career and my cultural identity, it becomes important to find constants to navigate with.

Xochitl, the pyramid, the Aztec's 20th day, is the constant, but Bermejo, the Spanish sailor who was first to see land from the bird's nest in 1492, a bloodthirsty conquistador's name, my grandfather's name, is the variable. Xochitl-Julisa Bermejo is the complex, multi-layered rainbow crowning my gondola. Though there will always be those frightened of my name and there will always be misspellings—Xochitl will be Xotchil or Xochilt—and the hyphen will shift places like hopscotch, I strive to find solace in the journey and not be ashamed to navigate the waters of my language and my name.

Cosecha

Pablo Miguel Martínez

the rains came

    in your mouth

        sprouted new words

cruise, lesion, out

    your hands jerked

        a grisaille of migrant

vine from hard ground—

    a queer season, ¿no?

        bent over beet—dirt-

crusted heart, the head

    of lettuce, too—this

        the work you were

born to do, mi'jo—every

    day the same, more

        rooting, every row

a retuning—psalmed

    fresa

sandía

    granada

    skin

flesh

    seed

Farmworker—conflation/the harsh throat of *work*—
is brown, is sweat, is dirt. No need for conjunction.
No place for jotos. Más allá, mariposas pollinating
wildflowers. Not efficient as abejas. A silent flutter,
no buzz. I hide who/what I am. Tight-leafed cabbage.
I straddle soft tufts, unending surcos of green whose
secrets I keep. The seeds, the roots, the pith. The skins
barely sheathe the seething, the rotting dreams, the pain.
Coséchame. Whispers blow through many-ringed trees
beyond these knowing fields. *Escúchame*, they tell me.

Dry mouth unending.
Sun-heat unrelenting.
Back ache unabating.

No. What am I saying?
I know what burns
there are in me:

the no-name ones,
the one-pata-here,
one-pata-there ones.

Once I believed
in sanctity; prayer
would save me, words

would save me. And then
I felt the sweet, unworded
press of a man's flesh

against mine. Against
all I knew. Again
and again I knew.

This, my soul, the *what*
I was born to do.

Spanish Ghazal

Barbara Brinson Curiel

The only language of loss left in the world is Arabic—
These words were said to me in a language not Arabic.

Aga Shahid Ali

Words for love, words for rage, words for heartbreak
pulse at the back of my mouth in Spanish.

For years it was the language of my best dreams
and lovers whispered cariñitos in my ear in Spanish.

Where is my homeland? The neighborhood
of my childhood was a canyon that echoed tender voices in Spanish.

Forbidden language, I learned to understand when my mother
and aunts told their secrets in Spanish.

Years of living among strangers has been a mallet
that crushed the clay slabs of my Spanish.

There have been days when words catch in my throat,
words unsaid in English or Spanish.

My children refused the burden of words to describe
our difference. They name themselves in English, not Spanish.

What does Barbara mean? Listen, it means Stranger
in English, Wild Woman in Spanish.

Gnarly Mexican Words
Desgranando La Lengua
Olga García Echeverría

> Her first step is to take inventory.
> *Despojando, desgranando, quitando paja.*
> Just what did she inherit from her ancestors?
>
> **Gloria Anzaldúa**

In the middle of the first grade, I was put into a "special" classroom reserved for monolingual Spanish speakers. The room was the size of a large walk-in closet and instead of regular desks and chairs, we sat on stools. In place of a blackboard, we had an easel with large writing pads. It was the mid 70s, and although the school, situated in East Los Angeles, had a student population primarily made up of Mexican and Mexican-American students, almost all of our teachers were white.

I don't recall the name of my teacher in that special classroom, but I do recall that she too was white. What was different about her was that she spoke to us in Anglo Spanish. "Boo-en-ohs dee-az. Komo eh-stan?" She meant well, I'm sure, but it sounded forced, distorted, and made us (the special kids) want to laugh. At home, I'd look into the mirror and practice my Anglo Spanish, "Me yamo Oh-ga. Eh-stoy en uu-nah class-eh deh pen-day-hoes."

The thing is that, although my parents were monolingual immigrants, I was, to quote Cheech and Chong's classic barrio song, "Born in East L.A." I understood and spoke English. What had unfortunately landed me into that classroom was a read-aloud where, out of panic and poor reading skills, I mangled Dick and Jane so badly that my teacher concluded that I did not speak English at all, but rather some alien tongue that belonged to another country. As a result, I was sent across the schoolyard into another class, where language misfits like me were housed.

Whereas at school, my literacy was labeled "special" (euphemism in my mind for deficient), language development at home was rich and flavored. Mexican Spanish was the mother tongue, the father tongue, the first tongue, but to say that it was the native tongue doesn't capture the whole picture. English from TV, older siblings, the streets, and school always seeped into my linguistic reality. English and Spanish in an interwoven tapestry were my real first tongue(s).

My parents were by no means bookish people. Having had little opportunity for formal schooling, their literacy in Spanish was limited. Still, language meals at home consisted of awesome words like bichi, pronounced bee-chee. This word partially explains why my father always called people he was pissed off at sonah-ba-bee-chees instead of son of a bitches. Bichi, however, means naked, not female dog. It comes from the Yaqui and its use is pretty common in the Northern state of Sonora, where my mother is from. There is even in the city of Nogales a colossal statue of a Yaqui bichi slaying the beast of ignorance. Whereas Europe has its famous nude dudes, David and The Thinker, Mexico has its enlightened encuerado, El Mono Bichi. But not everyone was pleased by the statue erection (no pun intended). The church and local religiosos at one point forced city leaders to put a giant diaper on El Mono Bichi. His exposed penis, huevos, and robust nachas offended, they claimed.

Like in Nogales, nakedness in our home also brought with it judgment and warnings. On *Sábado Gigante*, when women appeared a little too overexposed, my mother would note, "Mira nomás, andan todas bichis." Walking around todas bichis in public could attract the wrong kind of attention. To be too bichi in the fall or winter could lead to catching a cold or having aire enter the body. Bichi wasn't always bad, though. When Benny Hill ran fast-forward after bichi women in swimsuits, my mother cracked up laughing. British bichi, for some unknown reason, seemed to be less offensive than Latin American bichi.

Another common household word was lambiche, which means to be servile and connotes the verb lamer, to lick. If we begged for something or tried too hard to please, my father told us not to be lambiches, ass-lickers. One thing was to be poor and to want, but another was to appear desperate. To be a lambiche was disgraceful and showed a loss of dignity. There's no cultural honor in being a lambiche.

Salate was another awesome part of the lexicon. Whereas in some countries, salate means salad, in our home it meant ass. Someone with a large rump was said to have "un salate grande." When people offended my father, he'd send them to hell with, "¡Que me besen el salate!" This was equivalent to, "They can kiss my ass!" He also used salate to show reverence. For example, to express that Jack LaLanne was the king of exercise, my father would say, "Para a hacer ejercicio bésenle el salate a Yak LaLanne." Nalgas, nachas, and trasero were synonyms, but in our home the word salate, more rare and harsh sounding, assed-out all those other asses.

Alcahueta was another prized word. My father used it often because he liked to accuse women of covering up for other women. According to my father, the neighbor was an alcahueta because she let her teenage daughters date behind her husband's back. If the neighbor's husband reproached his wife about the daughters' whereabouts, the wife would innocently ask, "¿De qué hablas? Las muchachas andan en la biblioteca."

"¡Biblioteca! ¡Ha!" My father insisted that biblioteca was most likely alcahueta-code for day-time discoteca. "¡A mí no me hacen estúpido! Esas muchachas andan de voladas." My father, the omniscient narrator with a knack for hyperbole, could easily get riled up over scenarios and dialogues that he created in his head and reenacted in front of us.

My mother's annoyed classic response was, "¿Y tú cómo sabes?" It was a good question. How did my father know what was being discussed in the homes of neighbors who hardly ever spoke to us?

The word alcahueta has long intrigued me. In college, after taking my first Chicano History course, I erroneously imagined the word came from the Nahuatl because phonetically it conjures up other Mexican words that are Nahuatl in origin, such as cacahuate and aguacate. Yet, alcahueta isn't Nahuatl. It comes from the Arabic "al-qawwad" and means messenger, go-between, or a middle person for romantic or illicit activities. In short, an alcahueta (feminine) or alcahuete (masculine) will lie and cover up to help others "get it on." In the feminine, it can also mean a blabbermouth or gossiper. Even before knowing the etymology and full meaning of alcahueta, I knew (from how it was used in my home) that there was something subversive about it. I liked the idea of covering up for others, and even as a young girl I took pride in fooling my parents regularly. Whereas my father was so concerned with the doings of the neighbors, he didn't realize that his own household was full of sprouting alcahuetas.

My mother unfortunately lacked true alcahueta potential. It was impossible to get her to lie or cover up for anyone, so my three sisters and I lied to her too. In a home and culture where females had to be watched over and controlled, lest we ruin the family honor, we relied on each other to eke out a bit of freedom. When my two eldest sisters, Anna and Terry, claimed to be going to the movies with amigas from our church group, they took as escorts my sister Chuy and me. This seemed to please our parents, who conjured up memories of "the good old days" when girls and women in Mexico were constantly chaperoned.

Really, Anna and Terry had steady secret boyfriends who owned shiny Impala low-riders with hydraulics that made the cars bounce as they cruised down Whittier Boulevard. We'd leave the house as a pack of innocent girls, but once out of sight, we'd cackle like alcahueta witches, splitting up to our respective hangouts with schemes to meet up again at a set location and time. Alcahueta wasn't just a word to us; it was our underground railroad to hanging out, making out, cruising, plunging into the ocean in shorts and over-sized T-shirts. It was freedom to just be.

Philosophical concepts were also taught through words at home. Because of my father's tendency to bad-mouth others, my mother often referred to him as Mal Pensado, literally meaning the Bad Thinker, but culturally meaning he who has a lot of caca in his cabeza. A mal pensado sees things that aren't there and his view of reality is skewed towards the negative. Such was often the mental state of my father, and we were warned by our mother not to fall into the trap of being crippled by our own negative thoughts. "No hay que ser mal pensados," was a maternal mantra in our home that still echoes in my mind.

My mother's most fantastic name for my father, though, was cascarabias. When I'd asked her for permission to go somewhere or do something, she'd say, "Pregúntale a cascarabias." Cascarabias, I learned much later, is someone who is easily angered or always in a rancid mood. As a child, though, I didn't know this, yet I was drawn to this word that reminded me of two other words I did know in Spanish, "cascara" (rind or shell) and "rabia" (which could be either rabies or rage). I recall once as a young girl asking my mother what the word cascarabias actually meant.

"¿Apoco no sabes lo qué es cascarabias?" she said as she scrubbed clothes against the washboard in the laundry room.

I had heard the word for as long as I could remember, but I admitted. "No, no sé."

She looked at me in disbelief. Cascarabias was another one of those things we were just supposed to understand via DNA or genetic memory. "Pues, ¡un cascarabias es un cascarabias!" she said and continued scrubbing. Both my parents had the tendency to give definitions of unknown Spanish words using the very same words that needed explanation. When I stood there quietly, obviously still not getting it, she offered the following, "Cascarabias es tu papá. ¿No sabías eso?"

"Sí, pero qué *es* cascarabias?"

Finally, she paused her scrubbing and looked up, not at me, but at some faraway place only she could see. Her jaw tightened and her face contorted, "Pues, ¿qué más va ser?" There was spite in her usually spite-less voice. "¡Es el sebo del sebo!"

Depending on the translation, that could mean the fat of the fat, the lard of the lard, or the leftover-sucky-part of the leftover-sucky-part, but I understood without exactly knowing how I knew that what she meant by "el sebo del sebo" was the scum of the scum. The Ultimate Scum.

It was more than enough to satisfy me, but as my mother went back to her scrubbing, she added, "Un cascarabias es un viejo corrajudo y enfadoso, como tu padre."

I walked away from the laundry room that day dazzled, imagining my father as a growling creature made up of bubbling, putrid, foamy slime. Up until that moment I had thought that between my quarreling parents, my father was the champion of insults. His term of endearment for my mother was, after all, Molcas, short for molcajete, because he said that my mother, like the traditional grinding stone, spent her days chingando, chingando, y chingando.

Cascarabias. It sounded mythical and phantomish. It wasn't a curse word, but it was cathartic and hefty, and it could be used to insult and name the scrooges in my life. My father, who was prone to tantrums, could in fact at times be a cascarabias. The priest at our church, who never smiled and was always regañando (in particular the women), was a total cascarabias. I tucked the word cascarabias under my tongue that day and savored its power. It lives there still, wild and free, among so many other gnarly Mexican words that my parents fed me.

The Multiplicity of Language, Thought, and Experience
Adela Najarro

I have no memories of being tongue-tied in Spanish. Conversations came naturally with my Spanish-speaking grandmothers and with my aunts, uncles, and cousins. I did not discriminate between the two languages, since they were both available when needed. Hablaba con mis abuelitas, and then with my cousins too. Whichever language fit the occasion was fine, and I spoke what I spoke when I needed to speak. Looking back, Spanglish became the dominant language in the home and with my extended family. Everyone simply talked a lot in whatever way they knew best. In general, family members raised in Nicaragua remained Spanish dominant, while the children became English speakers. However, correcting grammar in either language was viewed as a highly obnoxious endeavor, and, thankfully, there were no grammar police on either side of the language line. Both languages, English and Spanish, were equally valued. My mother kept the connection to Nicaragua by telling stories in Spanish, the stories of her youth in Managua and León, as did my tías, tíos y esos primos who came to the States after the 1972 earthquake y la revolución. During my childhood, I was free to use the languages within me, naturally, effortlessly.

Often when thinking about language and its role in society, I think of the Indian fable of the blind men and the elephant. In the fable, each blind man attempts to describe the elephant by touching one body part; to the blind man holding the tail, the elephant is like a rope; to the blind man touching the leg, the elephant is like a tree trunk; to the one touching the side, the elephant is like a wall, and so on, etc. In regard to the various aspects of language, which captures the essence of the elephant? Taking a lesson from the fable, looking at only one aspect, such as speech, will not present the entire whole. Language is more than what is spoken, written, and read. Language is the vehicle by which we express experience to ourselves, to each other, and to the world. Depending on the circumstance, we talk, write, sing, pray, meditate, argue, contemplate, and more all about our experience as people on this planet. We begin in the home, in a culture, in a society, in the world, and it is through personal experience that we create the language we use.

My family's adaptation of language to include English with Spanish, and allow whatever speech came up to be spoken, relates to a general worldview arising out of hardship and the process of immigration. Moving from country to country, city to city, language to language fostered an acknowledgment that there is no one set way of doing things. Instead, flexibility is the only way to make it through, since what might come next cannot be contained or controlled, and in all likelihood will turn out to be unexpected. I can't imagine that my family's move to the States came with the expectation that they themselves, and their children, would end up speaking Spanglish, but we did, and the acceptance of Spanglish in my home became a way to acknowledge both Nicaragua and the States, and the fact that we were now part of two cultures with a variety of language strategies in our bodies, minds, and souls. I was raised with an acceptance of linguistic varieties in the home.

My family is composed of storytellers, not writers. Each and every one can tell a good tale that changes each time it's told. Considering the elephant, story-telling at times is considered somewhere back toward the hindquarters, while the written word is at the pinnacle between the ears. In a written document, experience has been made static, set, and confined to one telling, and I don't think my family was interested in fixating their stories. The fluidity of the verbal story sets it apart from the written page, and the members of my family all told stories of the this-and-that, along with what happened long ago, and yes, that one other thing, with the details, description, and analysis altering each time to fit the circumstances of the telling. At the heart of my family's mode of communication was an underlying perspective toward existence: that life was magical, a huge and grand adventure that did not need containment, where containment equated with futility since the day-to-day was not static, but in a constant state of change.

While attending outstanding California suburban schools, kindergarten through college, the push toward writing went beyond the instruction of grammatical rules and toward teaching a way of thinking, a particular way to organize thought, which demands linear connections from one step in the argument to the next, and so on toward a final conclusion. Organization. Argumentation. Documentation. The history of Western thought. That's what schools teach as "good" writing. Through being taught the writing processes, I was instructed in a particular way to think and experience the world from the minute I first stepped into a classroom, instructed in a way of thinking that clashed with my family's acceptance of the multiplicity of language and the fluctuating nature of human experience.

It was through poetry that I found the space to breathe and use language in a way that accepted my family's orientation that the world is fluctuating, chaotic, and beyond our desire for control. They accept whatever comes their way, be it Spanglish, be it a college graduate stuck on herself, be it new cities and cultures. This ability to live with impermeability, fluidity, and contradiction is imprinted at the core of my identity, and from there arises my dance with language and poetry. I have always written poems from the time I was a little girl, and I have always wondered why I was drawn to poetic forms. Now I think it is because poetry encourages non-linear thinking, the non-linear thinking characteristic of my family. In poetry, I found my voice because I was free from the constraints of the "right way" to do things. I could mix Spanish and English. I could go off on tangents. I could do whatever was needed to create the piece of art called a poem. Having given up the idea that linear thinking, and therefore linear writing, is the pinnacle of thought, I have come to believe that language is a web where the kitchen sink can be thrown in along with tortillas y carne asada as we make poems simply because we have to.

FAQ

Barbara Jane Reyes

1. *Are you fluent in your mother tongue? What is your mother tongue?*

I am fluent in the language of la luz, ang lakbay, el cruzamiento. My mother tongue is criollo y kimera; it is also mongrel and bastard. The tongue is not déficit but prisma, and it is the light which (in)forms root and offshoot de mi lengua. It is sometimes called refraction. Ang aking dila ay isang bahaghari, brillante.

Ina ko ay migrante, ang señora, ang doña. Ang kaniyang lenggwahe ay wikang casa, wikang esposa, wikang siyudad, wikang trabajo, y wikang mundo. Yes, I am fluent in my mother's tongue.

2. *Don't you worry that other people might not understand you?*

The ones who apprehend many meanings may alam na malikot ang diwa at hulog. They know una significado ay isang ilusyon (o di kaya, delusyon). The ones who demand understanding en una lengua only, the ones who demand isang hating dila, what they request is una violencia de la media lengua. They really want obediencia. Di ba? They want me to be their mono. Mga suplado. Ako po ay sigurado.

3. *Why are you so angry? Don't you ever smile?*

Why aren't you angry? Why does my outrage inconvenience you? Why is my resting bitch face your concern?

Are you afraid of me?

Who told you that a lady should always smile, and for whose benefit and pleasure would that be? Why did you believe them? Why do you believe them still?

4. *Why can't you just write about beautiful things?*

Voice is beautiful. Language is beautiful. Prayer is beautiful. Song is beautiful. Flight is beautiful. Home is beautiful. Daughter is beautiful. Grit is beautiful. Hope is beautiful.

Do you not see a woman fighting for air? Do you not see a woman guarding her kin? Do you not see a woman learning to speak? Do you not see a woman dreaming to be whole?

All of these are things of beauty. If you do not see the beauty in these, then I am sorry for you.

5. *Why don't you just say what you mean?*

I just did.

Mother Tongue

Suzy de Jesus Huerta

It is dusk and dinner is done. You are outside watering roses still in your purple work pumps and best jeans, Gloria Vanderbilt, indigo blue and unwrinkled. You can't stand the word *chola*, and hate the girls with the skinny eyebrows even more, but you creased and starched those jeans like a true *veterana*. You move on to sweep the gutter of dead leaves and fast-food wrappers. The sun has set and your silhouette against the dying light draws a whistle or two. I wonder what it feels like to have a man look at you that way. Not love. Not the way my father watches you. Not that way. I am stuck and thinking about what it is to be a woman and you turn to yell at me because I should be practicing the piano. On Saturday you will wake me early to accompany you to hand out flyers at Safeway. In cracked sentences, an English that mimics the music of your native tongue, you will explain the boycott to uncaring faces. You will cut them with questions like: "Do you know how these pesticides deform babies?" And you will grow loud and call them *cabrones y pendejos* e *hijos de la chingada* because you can't understand how not buying something is asking too much. I'll grow red with embarrassment but really I want to kick them in the shins for laughing in your face. You say, tonight they will eat those *pinche* grapes with cheese and wine. And my tired father, grey and dusted over in quarry dust, back in knots from a second shift at the Kaiser Cement Plant, will remind you to watch your language around the kids. Okay, okay, you will tell him, then turn to me with a wink while you squeeze his hands. But your mouth is a mother lode. From it, nearly thirty years later, I will learn how to say enough is enough.

Braided Soul

David Bowles

Before the monks came,
the original peoples
had three souls.

Teyolia—to use one of its names—was the spirit,
living on after death, released into paradise
and whatever lies beyond even that unknowable realm.

Ihiyotl was the breath, soul of emotions
and passions, the source of personal magic,
which shamans pooled and channeled.

Tonalli was created upon birth, congealing
from the divine energy that infused blood and brain,
capricious and slippery animal soul, often straying.

The monks shook their heads at this.
"One soul," they instructed. "El ánima.
Deposited in our flesh there in our mother's womb."

And as their culture and faith twist down the years
around those indigenous strands, we mestizo children
nod in growing epiphany sent from Dual God or Trinity—

There has always been one soul, just braided from the three.

Babel's Son

John Fry

Somewhere between if our lips meet and when.

Glimmers my ears see and my eyes hear.

*When I fall in love, I fall not only for him but the shimmers of the not-yet language
our mouths might make.*

As if a sky stretched throat to groin inside my skin.

He made my knees bend not in English, not in Spanish.

But where, and how, our lips met between them.

Any given poem holds a night sky's worth of constellations suspended in the frame of its attention.

What orients its expanse derives from an idiosyncratic combination of my wiring and what anchors me in space and time.

Cardinal directions: language(s), landscape(s), memory, desire.

Line of the horizon, line of the soul, line of the heart, line of the breath.

Given: that we are flesh.

If Christ is the Word made flesh, these words have flesh that your tongue can taste, your lips can kiss, your teeth can bite.

Given: that we are ensouled.

(Even if no one knows its exact location in the body.)

God: present, absent, the compass rose.

Born under the sign of Sagittarius a preacher's son on the day La Virgen de Guadalupe appeared to Juan Diego in the hills of Tepeyac, these orientations could be called a birthright.

Circa the Tower of Babel, all the world's languages were one tongue.

Everyone understood everyone before God shattered that understanding and scattered everyone and it throughout the world.

Supposedly because of ambition, pride.

Or so the story goes.

But what if the scattering was actually a blessing?

An invitation to connect *with*, to move *toward*.

Not despite differences.

Because of differences.

Each of us Jacob, though the angels we wrestle with have different names.

Angels of: otherness, spiritual homelessness, fear (not), south of the Nueces River and the Wild Horse Desert, his skin striking sparks against mine, his taste in my mouth.

Bibled from no lamb.

Baptized in the name of one.

I wrestle on/off the page, unwilling to go until I'm blessed.

Being from South Texas, negative capability *is* in ways Keats couldn't have imagined.

Anzaldúa didn't need to imagine it because she lived it.

She also gave it a better name.

Te extraño, I write toward my maternal grandmother gone wherever grandmothers go when they go.

Ahora y en la hora de su muerte.

La Virgen's face shining from the vela on my stove that entire evening.

Before I blew the candle out, I said a prayer.

Pero no dije la oración en Inglés.

I later learned that was the hour of her death.

I can say it in English.

"I miss you."

But I feel it, missing her, in ways English cannot.

Why do I miss my grandmother more in a language not her own than in the one that was?

Lately, I've been thinking about how we have multiple mothertongues.

How a mothertongue's mothertongue lives inside it, sometimes asleep, sometimes awake.

And how beautiful it is that in the world of that word used for the tongue we speak—this tongue that also speaks us—that it's given by a mother.

North American Christianity has nearly forgotten the mother who gave it the tongue it speaks (Catholicism aside).

Mexican-American Catholics, however, have forgotten neither that mother nor her names.

Even before I knew those names, for years I wrote in search of her.

Mother who gave me this tongue.

Discovered, long ago, Christ was called not only Lord and Savior but *Mother*.

Catholic in every way but name.

(Mother/Christ, have mercy on me.)

Ya te conozco, my lover says with his knowing grin.

Even if you aren't writing about God directly, you're still writing about God indirectly.

No, "the absence of" doesn't count.

You wrote a whole book about religion.

Isn't it time to give religion a rest.

Could I un-feel what my parents sang-said while I orbited like a star inside the galaxy of my mother.

Could I un-hear the words they whispered in my newborn ears.

Could I un-read the Bible stories that grew up with me.

Could I unfasten my skin for a skin unmarked by scripture.

Could I un-see the verses tattooed on the insides of my eyelids.

Under every mothertongue, another mothertongue.

Nothing is ever no thing.

If you're spiritually inclined—

The tongue in the mouth of Christianity's mother knows this.

Previously, I've written about the weather patterns of the soul in terms of the landscape around me, but I don't want to use the weather outside my window to forecast the chances of rain inside my skin anymore.

I want to write about the weather because it's the weather:

That July when I leaned in to lick some of the salt off his neck.

Night wind on our faces.

How unabashedly biblical it was.

What my tongue traced on my beloved's back, a song of songs.

Often I've wished I could simply walk away from Christianity and, for a decade, tried.

Heresy had proven hell, a halfway house I was dying in, so I took off the sackcloth and ashes as I walked out the door, hoping apostasy would prove more bearable.

When wandering in the wilderness, nakedness can prove deadly.

This is as metaphysically true as it would be walking naked in the deserts of the Holy Land.

Because Jesus wandered for forty days in one, the Christian wilderness is always a desert.

Throughout my twenties, my body lived in various Texan towns.

A desert lived inside of me.

And wherever I went, Christianity went with me.

What sounds truer in Spanish than in English.

Hermoso.

Te quiero.

Intertwined, we're when dawn meets dusk.

Even though what wheels above our heads doesn't reflect this phenomenon.

Even though light pollution in Austin where I live, where he lives in San Antonio, sets the cloud-covered horizon on fire day or night.

Whether I walked far afield or outside entirely the faith in question.

(When is faith not question and/or doubt.)

Saying fuck you yet again felt, finally, too easy.

So in the words of the religion given me, with and against the words of the religion given me, I began to write poems that reckoned and reconciled with what I'd been given as a child.

A language as fractured as it had once fractured me.

(I don't know if it's possible for a wound to be linguistic, but I wrote into and out of such a space as if it were.)

A prodigal's prayerbook written with as many tongues as the Bible does.

In that book of bewilderment, a litany of biblical figures—not dramatic monologues so much as self-portraits—speak.

My voice channels theirs, but their voices equally channel mine.

(Eve, Isaac, Samuel, Jonah, Mary, Lazarus, the man from whom Christ casts the demon Legion out, Judas.)

Their stories, the underneath of mine.

Writing them required walking into a thicket of words where more than just one world is, where this is always more than one kind of time.

English wasn't the only language whispered in my ears as I formed my first words.

Three times a week or more—and for hours at a time—Elva cared for me in the nursery while my parents were at church in Alice, Tejas.

Memory, for me, began after my family left Alice, so I know this only secondhand.

Six months old to a year and a half.

Mijo, she called me, her baby.

Elva spoke English haltingly.

I imagine, because I can only imagine, her Spanish was unadulterated song.

Is she why English isn't the only language where and when I feel that I am home?

I've tried to find her, but it was the early 1980s and the church has no records of her.

Elva, I called when walking up to the church, Elva, it's John.

Elva, (wherever you are), it's John.

Having no memories of her, I believe the Spanish moving through me does remember her when I speak it.

Tongue she gave me.

Creo que el Español la recuerda cuando yo hablo el lenguaje que me dio.

I write to honor each of the mothers who gave me the tongues I speak.

Elva is one of her names.

Writing this queer breviary hasn't diminished the fact that I remain bewildered by what's wondrous and passing strange.

Child of the Word who moves through the worlds in and with words.

Poetry: where worlds and languages touch.

After years of chronicling pilgrimage in terms of the other world of biblical time, I now want the ground beneath my feet to be the ground beneath my words.

I may never not be writing about what happens when spirituality and (homo) sexuality get into bed together the way I sleep next to my beloved.

But when I do, I strive to chronicle it in ways that rouse the two words asleep inside bewilderment: *be wilder*.

If, now, I were to write what David whispered into Jonathan's ear as they made love, their skin-to-skin psalm unsung by any tongue in the Bible would sound like the selah of when he enters me, when I enter him.

Somewhere entre English y Español.

Because one tongue will never be enough.

The Bringing Forth

Kim Shuck

Because creating gods is
Surgery
Carving in
Flesh
Sculpting the self with
Chisels made of chipped words the
Black glass of words that
Shimmers on the edges
Cuts clean

Because making new myths takes
Practice
Thumb polished
Idea
Rubbed smooth
Day and day and the
Black glass of imagination
Buried to lead us
Back

Dream well
Dream wide
Dream generous

Contributor Biographies

EDITORS

ire'ne lara silva is the author of *furia* (poetry, Mouthfeel Press, 2010) which received an Honorable Mention for the 2011 International Latino Book Award and *flesh to bone* (short stories, Aunt Lute Books, 2013) which won the 2013 Premio Aztlán, placed 2nd for the 2014 NACCS Tejas Foco Award for Fiction, and was a finalist for Foreward Review's Book of the Year Award in Multicultural Fiction. Her most recent collection of poetry, *blood sugar canto*, was published by Saddle Road Press in January 2016. ire'ne is the recipient of the 2014 Alfredo Cisneros del Moral Award, the Fiction Finalist for AROHO's 2013 Gift of Freedom Award, and the 2008 recipient of the Gloria Anzaldúa Milagro Award, as well as a Macondo Workshop member and CantoMundo Inaugural Fellow. She and Moises S. L. Lara are currently co-coordinators for the Flor De Nopal Literary Festival.

Dan Vera is a writer, editor, and literary historian. The author of two poetry collections, *Speaking Wiri Wiri*, inaugural winner of the Letras Latinas/Red Hen Poetry Prize, and *The Space Between Our Danger and Delight*, his work has appeared in various publications and university curricula. He's been awarded residency fellowships at the Virginia Center for the Creative Arts, Soul Mountain Retreat, and Ragdale Foundation. *Latino Stories* recognized him as a Top Ten "New" Latino Author to Watch (and Read), calling him "a talented, sophisticated poet who is a master at playing with words." His watercolors have been featured in literary journals and book covers. Co-curator of the literary history site DC Writers' Homes, he publishes other authors through Poetry Mutual Press and Souvenir Spoon Books and chairs the Split This Rock Poetry board. He lives in Washington, DC, with his husband Peter and their dog Blossom Dearie. For more, visit http://www.danvera.com.

CONTRIBUTORS

Melanie Márquez Adams was born and raised in the coastal city of Guayaquil, Ecuador. Her work has appeared in the anthologies *We crossed the line* (Abismos, 2015), *Microrrelatos de amor* (Brevilla, 2016), and *Minimalismos 2*, a flash fiction collection published in Argentina. She has work published in *The Acentos Review*, *Literal: Latin American Voices*, *ViceVersa*, and *El BeiSMan*, among others. Márquez Adams holds an MA in Liberal Studies and is editing an anthology of Andean literature in the US, titled *Al Norte de la Cordillera*, to be published by New York–based SonicerJ this fall. You can visit her at www.melaniemarquezadams.com.

Allen Baros is a queer Chicano from the South Valley of Albuquerque, New Mexico. He is a writer, scholar, and teacher at the University of Washington, where he is completing his PhD dissertation about family, intimacy, and personhood in Chican@ culture. Among his favorite things to write about are how people know and understand the world from queer and ethnic perspectives and use those ways of knowing to reimagine and recreate themselves, their families, their communities, and their world. Currently he lives in Seattle, Washington with his partner Nigel and their two pit bulls.

Cordelia Barrera, Associate Professor of English at Texas Tech University, received her PhD at the University of Texas, San Antonio. She specializes in Latin@ literatures, the American Southwest, and Third Space feminism. Her publications have appeared in *The Quarterly Review of Film and Video*, *Western American Literature*, and *Chicana/Latina Studies: The Journal of MALCS*. Her work highlights the need to disrupt mythologies of the American West by incorporating border voices and identities, and concentrates on the literature of social justice and the environment.

Nidia Melissa Bautista is a traveler, journalist, and perpetual student of the barrios of Boyle Heights and Mexico City. As mujer y amante transfronteriza, her earliest journeys began with her parents, who, in their move from their rural roots in northern Mexico to Los Angeles, wove the lessons and walkways that articulated the transbarrio and bordered existence she came to call home. Her current journey is centered on exploring various literary forms and structures, as she familiarizes herself with both words of flesh and experience, learning to be simultaneously thinker and poet. To follow her journeys, read her at ellaestaporembarcar.com.

Xochitl-Julisa Bermejo is a 2016–2017 Steinbeck Fellow, 2015 Barbara Deming Fund grantee, and the 2013 Poets & Writers California Writers Exchange Award poetry winner. She has work published in *Acentos Review*, *CALYX*, *crazyhorse*, and *The James Franco Review*, among others. A short dramatization of her poem "Our Lady of the Water Gallons," directed by Jesús Salvador Treviño, can be viewed at latinopia.com. She curates the reading series HITCHED and cofounded Women Who Submit. Her debut poetry collection, *Built with Safe Spaces* (Sundress Publications 2016), is partly inspired by her work with the Tucson-based organization No More Deaths.

Tara Betts is the author of *Break the Habit* and *Arc & Hue*. Her chapbooks include *Never Been Lois Lane*, *7 x 7: kwansabas*, and *THE GREATEST!: An Homage to Muhammad Ali*. Her writing has appeared in *POETRY*, *Essence*,

HBO's "Def Poetry Jam," and other journals and anthologies. She teaches at University of Illinois–Chicago.

David Bowles is a Mexican-American author from the Río Grande Valley of south Texas, where he teaches at the University of Texas. Recipient of awards from the American Library Association, Texas Institute of Letters, and Texas Associated Press, he has written several books, among them *Flower, Song, Dance: Aztec and Maya Poetry* and Pura Belpré winner *The Smoking Mirror*. Additionally, his work has been published in venues including *Rattle*, *Strange Horizons*, *Apex Magazine*, *Metamorphoses*, *Translation Review*, *The Langdon Review of the Arts in Texas*, *Huizache*, *Axolotl*, *Concho River Review*, *Eye to the Telescope*, *Asymptote*, and *BorderSenses*.

Carmen Calatayud is the author of *In the Company of Spirits*, which was a runner-up for the Walt Whitman Award, given by the Academy of American Poets. Her poetry most recently appears in the anthology *Poetry of Resistance: Voices for Social Justice*. Her writing has garnered a Best of La Bloga award and a Larry Neal Poetry Award. For five years, Carmen was a poet moderator for Poets Responding to SB 1070, a Facebook group created by the late Francisco X. Alarcón that features poetry and news about Arizona's racial profiling immigration law and other human rights news.

Abigail Carl-Klassen was raised in rural west Texas and radicalized on the US-Mexico border. Her work has appeared in *Cimarron Review*, *Guernica*, *Aster(ix)*, and *Post Road*, among others, and was nominated for a Pushcart Prize and Best New Poets 2015. She earned an MFA from the University of Texas at El Paso's Bilingual Creative Writing Program and taught at El Paso Community College and the University of Texas at El Paso. Before becoming a college instructor, she worked in community development and in the El Paso public schools.

Sarah A. Chavez, a mestiza born and raised in the California Central Valley, is the author of the chapbook *All Day, Talking* (Dancing Girl Press, 2014), a selection of which won the Susan Atefat Peckham Fellowship (2013). Her debut full-length poetry collection, *Hands That Break & Scar*, is forthcoming from Sundress Publications (2017). She holds a PhD in English from the University of Nebraska–Lincoln and is a Visiting Assistant Professor teaching Ethnic American literature and creative writing at Marshall University. She is a proud member of the Macondo Writers Workshop. www.sarahachavez.com

D.M. Chávez is a science writer and tech editor by trade. Of Apache, Aztec, Navajo, and European descents, she practices contemplative meditation and travels to remote places to photograph and write about the wild she encounters there, including many two-leggeds. Her poetry has been published in literary magazines and journals, nominated for a Pushcart, and excerpted in a book about the writing craft. The narrative poem "White Dog, Femur Shrinking" also appears in Diane's work in progress: *BREAD PUDDING POEMS from Tributaries Converging.* She occasionally blogs at dmsolis.blogspot.com and can always be messaged via facebook.com/dmsolis.solis1.

Karla Cordero is the recipient of the Spoken Word Immersion Fellowship for writers of color from The Loft Literary Center and recipient of the Global Diversity Award at San Diego State University. Cordero curates Voice For Change, a reading series inviting writers to share narratives on survival. She is a contributing writer for *Poetry International* and the founder and editor of *Spit Journal*, an online literary review for poetry and social justice. Cordero's work has been published in *The Acentos Review, Word Riot, Toe Good Poetry*, and elsewhere. Her chapbook, *Grasshoppers Before Gods* (2016), was published by Dancing Girl Press.

Barbara Brinson Curiel's book *Mexican Jenny and Other Poems* won the 2012 Philip Levine prize and was published in 2014 by Anhinga Press. She has published poems in the journals *Kweli, Huizsache,* and *The Acentos Review.* Her poems are included in the collection *Cantar de Espejos: Poesía Testimonial Chicana por Mujeres* published in Mexico, as well as in other anthologies. Barbara is a member of the coordinating committee of CantoMundo, the national organization for Latina/o poets. She is also a professor in the departments of Critical Race, Gender, and Sexuality Studies and English at Humboldt State University.

César L. De León resides in McAllen, Texas. His poetry is included in the anthologies *Along the River 2: More Voices From the Rio Grande,* and *Juventud!: Growing up on the Border,* among other anthologies and journals. In 2012, César received a Golden Circle Award from the University of Columbia Press for his poem "Us," and in 2014 he was awarded 2nd place in poetry from the Texas Intercollegiate Press Association. He is an MFA candidate in Creative Writing with a Certificate in Mexican American Studies at the University of Texas–Rio Grande Valley.

Originally from South Texas, **John Fry** is the author of the poetry chapbook *silt will swirl* (NewBorder). His poems have appeared in in *Waxwing, Colorado Review, West Branch, Blackbird,* and *Borderlands,* among others. He's a graduate of Texas State University's MFA program and a poetry editor for *Newfound Journal.* He lives and writes in Austin—where he's pursuing a PhD in medieval English literature at the University of Texas—and, whenever possible, he follows the highway's heart line to where his lives in San Antonio.

Olga García Echeverría is the author of *Falling Angels: Cuentos y Poemas.* Her work appears in *Lavandería: A Mixed Load of Women, Wash, and Words, U.S. Latino Literature Today, Telling Tongues: A Latin@ Anthology on Language, Bird Float / Tree Song, The Sun Magazine,* and is forthcoming in *Jota* by Kórima Press. She was selected by A Room of Her Own (AROHO) as the 2013 Touching

Lives Fellow, and in the spring of 2015 she was a finalist for AROHO's Orlando Literary Prize in the genre of Creative Non-fiction. She lives, teaches, and shape-shifts in Los Angeles.

Rodney Gomez is the author of the chapbooks *Mouth Filled with Night* (Northwestern University Press, 2014) and *Spine* (Newfound, 2015). His work has received the Drinking Gourd Poetry Prize, the Gloria Anzaldúa Prize, and the RHINO Editors' Prize. His poems appear in *Denver Quarterly*, *Barrow Street*, *Pleiades*, *Salt Hill*, *Diode*, and other journals. He lives and works in the lower Rio Grande Valley of Texas.

New Jersey native **Ysabel Y. González** is also known for her performance poetry under the alias Ancestral Poetisa. She received her BA from Rutgers University, an MFA in Poetry from Drew University, and works for the Poetry Program at the Geraldine R. Dodge Foundation. Ysabel has received invitations to attend VONA, Tin House, Ashbery Home School and BOAAT Press writing workshops. She is also the Program Director for the BOAAT Writing Retreat and has been published in *The Wide Shore*, *Waxwing Literary Journal*, *Huizache*, *Acentos Review*, and *phati'tude Literary Magazine*. Find more of her poems and recorded performances at www.ysabelgonzalez.com.

Alexis Pauline Gumbs is the granddaughter of Lydia May Gumbs, designer of the revolutionary flag of Anguilla. Alexis is the co-editor of *Revolutionary Mothering: Love on the Front Lines*, an anthology in the tradition of *This Bridge Called My Back*. She is also the author of *Spill: Scenes of Black Feminist Fugitivity* and the founder of the Eternal Summer of the Black Feminist Mind Community School in Durham, North Carolina and the co-founder of the Mobile Homecoming Project, an experiential archive amplifying generations of Black LGBTQ Brilliance.

Roy G. Guzmán was born in Honduras and raised in Miami. He is an MFA candidate in creative writing at the University of Minnesota. His work has appeared or will appear in *The Adroit Journal*, *Breakwater Review*, *Word Riot*, *Reservoir*, *Connotation Press*, and *Notre Dame Review*. Roy is the poetry editor for *Sundog Lit*, and the recipient of a Pushcart prize nomination and a Gesell Award honorable mention in fiction. This summer, he will serve as the Scribe for Human Rights at the University of Minnesota, focusing on issues affecting migrant farm workers.

Minal Hajratwala (www.minalhajratwala.com) is author of the award-winning epic *Leaving India: My Family's Journey from Five Villages to Five Continents* (2009), which was called "incomparable" by Alice Walker and "searingly honest" by the Washington Post, and editor of *Out! Stories from the New Queer India* (2013). Her latest book is *Bountiful Instructions for Enlightenment*, published by The (Great) Indian Poetry Collective, a mentorship-model press of which she is a co-founder. She graduated from Stanford University, was a fellow at Columbia

University, and was a 2011 Fulbright-Nehru Senior Scholar. As a writing coach and founder of Write Like a Unicorn, she loves helping writers to give voice and shape to their untold stories.

Inés Hernández-Avila, Nimipu (Nez Perce)/Tejana, is Professor of Native American Studies at UC Davis, a scholar, poet, and visual artist. Her most recent publication is *Entre Guadalupe y Malinche: Tejanas in Literature and Art* (University of Texas Press, 2016), co-edited with Norma E. Cantú. She's held artist's residencies at Headlands Center for the Arts (Sausalito), Centrum (Port Townsend), and New Pacific Studios (Mt. Bruce, New Zealand). She is completing work on a collection of contemporary Mayan poetry from Chiapas. The poems will appear in the indigenous languages of the poets, in Spanish, and in English, with her translations and her introduction.

Suzy de Jesus Huerta is a composition writing professor and poet from San Jose, California. She dedicates most of her energy to the California community college system and its inspiring student body. She is a two-time VONA alumna (2010, 2012). Suzy is proud to curate the new reading series Oakland Crossroads, which she co-founded at Studio Grand in Oakland, California. Her work has appeared in *La Bloga, The Packinghouse Review, Poets Responding to SB1070, Bordersenses, Poetry of Resistance: A Multicultural Anthology in Response to Arizona SB 1070, Xenophobia, and Injustice*, and other journals. She lives in San Francisco.

Joe Jiménez is the author of *The Possibilities of Mud* (Kórima 2014) and *Bloodline* (Arte Público 2016). Jiménez is the recipient of the 2016 Letras Latinas/Red Hen Press Poetry Prize. He lives in San Antonio, Texas, where he teaches at Thomas Jefferson High School and is a member of the Macondo Writing Workshops. For more information, visit joejimenez.net.

Pablo Miguel Martínez's collection of poems, *Brazos, Carry Me*, received the 2013 PEN Southwest Book Award for Poetry. Writing in the *San Francisco Chronicle*, Sandra Cisneros praised it as her favorite book of 2013. His chapbook, *Cuent@*, was published by Finishing Line Press in March 2016. Martínez's work has appeared in numerous publications. He has been a recipient of the Chicano/Latino Literary Prize, among other awards. His literary work has received support from the Alfredo Cisneros Del Moral Foundation and the Artist Foundation of San Antonio. He is a co-founder of CantoMundo, a national retreat-workshop for Latina/o poets.

Rachel McKibbens is a two-time New York Foundation for the Arts poetry fellow and author of the poetry collections *Into the Dark & Emptying Field* (2013), *Pink Elephant* (2009), and the chapbook *MAMMOTH*. Her poems, short stories, and essays have been featured in numerous journals and blogs, including *The Academy of American Poets Poem-a-Day, VIDA: Her Kind, The Los Angeles Review, The Huffington Post, The Acentos Review, PANK, The Nervous*

Breakdown, and *The Collagist*. McKibbens is also the founder of Pink Door, a writing retreat exclusively for women of color.

Lupe Mendez is a poet/educator/activist, CantoMundo Fellow, founder of Tintero Projects, and co-founder of the Librotraficante Movement. Lupe works with Nuestra Palabra: Latino Writers Having Their Say, Tintero Projects, and the Brazilian Arts Foundation to promote poetry events, advocate for literacy/ literature, and organize creative writing workshops that are open to the public. He holds an MFA from the University of Texas at El Paso and a 2012 co-winner of the Downs Intellectual Freedom Award. He lives in Houston, TX.

Tomas Moniz is the founder, editor, and writer for the award winning zine, book, and magazine: *Rad Dad*. His novella *Bellies and Buffalos* is a tender, chaotic road trip about friendship, family and Flamin' Hot Cheetos. He is co-founder and co-host of the rambunctious monthly reading series Saturday Night Special in Berkeley. He's been making zines since the late nineties, and his most current zine *addition / subtraction* is available, but you have to write him a postcard: PO Box 3555, Berkeley, CA 94703. He promises to write back.

Juan Morales is the author of the poetry collections *The Siren World*, *Friday and the Year That Followed*, and the forthcoming collection *The Handyman's Guide to End Times*. His poems also recently appeared in *Poet Lore*, *Hayden's Ferry Review*, *Más Tequila Review*, *PANK*, and *Duende*. He is a CantoMundo Fellow, the editor of *Pilgrimage Magazine*, and an Associate Professor of English at Colorado State University–Pueblo, where he directs the Creative Writing Program and curates the SoCo Reading Series.

Miguel M. Morales grew up in Texas working as a migrant/seasonal farmworker and child laborer. He is a Lambda Literary Fellow and an alum of VONA/Voices and the Macondo Writers' Workshop. He also serves as president of the Latino Writers Collective. Additionally, Miguel co-hosts *The Tenth Voice*, an LGBTQ radio magazine, on KKFI 90.1FM. His work appears in *Primera Página: Poetry from the Latino Heartland*, *Cuentos del Centro: Stories from the Latino Heartland*, *From Macho to Mariposa: New Gay Latino Fiction*, *Hibernation and Other Poems by Bear Bards*, in *Pilgrimage* and *Raspa* magazines, *Duende Journal*, and *Borderlands: Texas Poetry Review*.

Adela Najarro is the author of two poetry collections: *Split Geography* and *Twice Told Over*. She currently teaches creative writing, literature, and composition at Cabrillo College. As the English instructor for the Puente Project, a program designed to support Latinidad in all its aspects, she works toward preparing community college students to transfer to four-year colleges and universities. Her extended family's emigration from Nicaragua to San Francisco began in the 1940s and concluded in the eighties when the last of the family settled in the Los Angeles area. She now calls Santa Cruz, California home.

Cecca Austin Ochoa serves as Managing Editor for *Apogee Journal*. Her fiction has appeared or is forthcoming in *Art XX, MAKE: Literary Magazine, Kweli Journal, Nat. Brut,* and anthologized in *Pariahs* (SFA Press). She is a 2014 alumnus of Voices of Our Nation's Artists. In 2011, she received the Astraea Foundation's Lesbian Writer's Award.

Shauna Osborn is a Numunuu (Comanche)/German mestiza artist, researcher, and wordsmith. She has earned a BA from the University of Oklahoma and an MFA from New Mexico State University. Her debut poetry collection, *Arachnid Verve,* focuses on the acrobatic nature of Southwestern life. Shauna's list of honors includes a 2015 Artist in Residence for A Room of Her Own Foundation's Waves Writing Retreat, a National Poetry Award from the New York Public Library, Alternating Current Press Luminaire Award for Best Poetry, and the Native Writer Award from UNM Summer Writers' Conference. You can find her work online at shaunamosborn.wordpress.com.

Monica Palacios is the creator of solo shows, plays, screenplays, short stories, stand-up comedy, poems, essays, and blogs featuring the Latina/o LGBTQ experience. National and international scholars have critically engaged her work in academic journals, books, dissertations, and conference panels. Palacios was awarded a Postdoctoral Rockefeller Fellowship and is a highly anthologized writer. Los Angeles Mayor Antonio Villaraigosa honored Monica for three decades of groundbreaking Chicana lesbian performance. Monica has taught at CSU Long Beach, UCLA, UC Santa Barbara, UC Riverside, Loyola Marymount University, Claremont College, Pomona College, CSU Los Angeles, and American Academy of Dramatic Arts. www.monicapalacios.com

Victor Payan is an award-winning writer, multidisciplinary artist, and arts administrator whose work promotes tolerance, understanding, and community empowerment. He is author of the "Keep on Crossin' Manifesto" and co-creator of the Keep on Crossin' movement. He collaborates with Pocha Peña on the lucha libre–inspired project Aztec Gold and is a founding member of the Taco Shop Poets. He is also an accomplished humorist and satirist. His latest projects are Mexistentialism and LAFTA, the Latin American Free Thought Agreement. He divides his time between California, Texas, and anywhere there is a border that needs crossing. His website is victorpayan.com.

Emmy Pérez is the author of *With the River on Our Face* (University of Arizona Press) and *Solstice* (Swan Scythe Press). Originally from Santa Ana, California, she has lived on the Texas-Mexico border, from El Paso to the Rio Grande Valley, since the year 2000. A graduate of Columbia University and the University of Southern California, she is a member of the Macondo Writers' Workshop founded by Sandra Cisneros. Currently, she is an associate professor at the University of Texas Rio Grande Valley, where she founded (in 2008) an annual event she coordinates: "El Retorno: El Valle Celebra Nuestra Gloria Anzaldúa."

Gabriela Ramirez-Chavez holds a BA in English Literature and Creative Writing from California State University, Long Beach. Her work has appeared or is forthcoming in Third Woman Press's inaugural anthology, *The Acentos Review*, *Kweli*, *Plath Profiles*, and elsewhere. She is currently pursuing a PhD in Literature with a Creative/Critical Writing concentration at University of California, Santa Cruz, where she focuses on 20th century and contemporary Latina/o literature, experimental poetics, and cross-genre texts. As part of her dissertation, she is also writing a collection about her maternal uncle's disappearance from Guatemala in the early 1980s.

Barbara Jane Reyes is the author of *To Love as Aswang*. She was born in Manila, Philippines, raised in the San Francisco Bay Area, and is the author of three previous collections of poetry, *Gravities of Center*, *Poeta en San Francisco*, which received the James Laughlin Award of the Academy of American Poets, and *Diwata*, which received the Global Filipino Literary Award for Poetry. Her fifth book, *Invocation to Daughters*, is forthcoming from City Lights Publishing.

jo reyes-boitel: writer, motivator/supporter, mother, daughter to oya and obatala, rabid music listener, percussionist and lover. texas transplant, by way of minnesota | florida | mexico | cuba.

Elsie Rivas Gómez was born in El Salvador and raised in the San Francisco Bay Area. She now teaches and writes in Pasadena, California. Recently, her work has been included in *Theatre Under My Skin, Contemporary Salvadoran Poetry / Teatro Bajo Mi Piel, Poesía Salvadoreña Contemporanea*, and the annual Mujeres de Maiz Zine, Vol. 14, *ONE: Body, Mind, Spirit*. Her chapbook *Swimming in El Rio Sumpul* was nominated for the Pushcart Prize.

José Antonio Rodríguez is the author of the poetry collections *The Shallow End of Sleep* and *Backlit Hour*, and the forthcoming memoir *House Built on Ashes* (University of Oklahoma Press). He's poetry editor of *riverSedge* and a fellow of CantoMundo and Macondo and teaches writing at the University of Texas–Rio Grande Valley.

Born and raised in Lebanon, **Nadine Saliba** spent her childhood summers in Syria visiting her mother's family. In the midst of the Lebanese civil war, her parents applied for immigration to the United States. She has an MA in Politics with a focus on Political Theory and International Relations. She works as a freelance translator and has published essays on the politics of Western Asia and women's issues. After 9/11, she helped found the San Antonio chapter of the American-Arab Anti-Discrimination Committee (ADC) and is a board member of the Esperanza Peace and Justice Center.

Veronica Sandoval is Lady Mariposa, a poet sCHOLAr for the Rio Grande Valle, Tejas. She has a spoken word album entitled *Hecha en El Valle: Spoken Word & Borderland Beats*. Her poetry has appeared in various anthologies and publications including: Aunt Lute Press, VAO Publishing, Lamar University, Savant Books & Publications, El Zarape Press, *Revista Literaria De El Tecolote*, and Texas A&M University Press. She is currently a graduate student at Washington State University working on a PhD in American Studies. She is an academic chola whose research interests include chola agency, history, cultural productions & the Chola Pinup Network.

T. Sarmina is a queer xicanx poet born and raised in the boiling belly of California—the San Joaquin Valley. Their work is rooted in three places they've called home: Porterville, Oakland, and Los Angeles. Their poetry focuses on how bodies of diaspora navigate and find home in liminal spaces. They have been published in *Coiled Serpent* (Tia Chucha Press), *Dryland Lit*, and *In the Words of Womyn* (Yellow Chair Press). They currently work as the Writers' Room Coordinator at 826LA, where they help high school students publish their narratives and poetry.

Kim Shuck's first manuscript won the Native Writer's Circle of the Americas Diane Decorah award in 2005. Since then, she's won a Mary Tall Mountain Award, published two full books of poetry, one poetry chapbook, and a book of vignette fiction. Shuck performs and curates poetry readings in and around San Francisco, most notably the Gears Turning Poetry Series and a special event at the Beat Museum. She teaches poetry, talks about poetry, and writes piles of poems. Her most recent book is *Clouds Running In* from Taurean Horn Press.

Daniel E. Solís y Martínez is a Salvadoreño/American community-based educator and writer born and raised in Los Angeles. Dedicated to nurturing youth to grow into transformative healers and nepantlerxs in the here and now, Solís y Martínez works to build youth-led movements for justice and liberation. Solís y Martínez is also active in grassroots herbal medicine work, and self-publishes *Quercus Agrifolia*, an anti-oppression herbalism zine. Solís y Martínez's writing has been published in the online anthology *BeyondMasculinity*, *Readings for Diversity & Social Justice, 2nd Edition*, and *BlackGirlDangerous*.

David Hatfield Sparks is a writer, musician, and gay father who has been active in queer multicultural communities from the Midwest and Manhattan to Austin, Texas, and San Francisco. He and his husband Randy P. Conner were original participants in the "El Mundo Zurdo" performance series in San Francisco. His poems and essays have appeared in feminist and LGBTQ publications, including the anthology *She Is Everywhere* (vol. 3, 2012), *Witches and Pagans* magazine (no. 29, 2015), and the forthcoming *El Mundo Zurdo V*. His poetry book *Princes and Pumpkins* won 1st Prize in the 2015 Writer's Digest Poetry e-Book Contest.

A Michoacán native raised in California's Central Valley, **Oswaldo Vargas** is a 23-year-old student attending the University of California, Davis and majoring in History. It was at UC Davis where professor and fellow *Imaniman* contributor